The University Through the Eyes of Faith

Steve Moore, editor

Timothy M. Beuthin, consulting editor

THE UNIVERSITY THROUGH THE EYES OF FAITH
Steve Moore, editor
Timothy M. Beuthin, consulting editor

ISBN 0-89367-228-9

©1998
Light and Life Communications
Indianapolis, IN 46253-5002
Printed in the U.S.A.

"The pressures of contemporary secular thinking have threatened to obliterate the historic alliance of the Christian religion and liberal education. This exciting work revives this vital relationship between faith and learning in a manner that respects both spiritual truth and the changing era for which it must be newly described."

Earl G. Hunt Jr.
President
The Foundation for Evangelism

"This book is a much-needed apologetic for Christian higher education. It will be read with special interest by academicians questioning the role of the Christian college and university in our times. I especially recommend it to young Christian faculty members whether they are in Christian or secular institutions, for it provides a philosophical foundation for a lifetime of service to Christ and His kingdom. This book may replace Holmes' *The Idea of a Christian College* as a must-read for scholars in the Christian academy."

Samuel Dunn
Vice President for Academic Affairs
Northwest Nazarene College

"Steve Moore has affirmed the dream and articulated the role of the church-related college and university at the turn of this century. His perspectives are enriched by the inside views and breadth of experience represented by him and his contributors. This is a strategic book at a strategic time."

Leslie Parrott Sr.
President Emeritus
Olivet Nazarene University

Contents

Contributors Biographies:

Dr. Steve Moore, vice president for campus life at Seattle Pacific University, earned his Ph.D. from the University of Michigan and is an alumnus of McMurry University, Asbury Theological Seminary and St. Andrew's University (Scotland). He recently completed post-graduate study at Harvard University and was a visiting scholar at Oxford University. Moore has authored numerous articles and books and is a frequent speaker on U.S. campuses.

Dr. William Hull, former provost of Samford University in Birmingham, AL, now serves as the institution's "University Professor." He helps equip faculty members in the integration of faith with their academic disciplines. Hull also is an author, an ordained Baptist minister, has pastored several churches, and lectures widely on higher education's relationship to the life of the church.

Dr. Earl Palmer is the senior pastor of University Presbyterian Church, Seattle, WA. Palmer has authored numerous books and is a widely sought-after Bible teacher. He currently serves on the boards of both Princeton University Divinity School and Whitworth College.

Dr. Harold Heie is director for the Center for Christian Studies at Gordon College and a senior fellow at the Coalition for Christian Colleges and Universities. He formerly served as vice president of academic affairs at Messiah College. Heie is frequently recognized as one of the outstanding leaders among faculty in U.S. liberal arts colleges.

Dr. Philip Eaton, president of Seattle Pacific University, previously served for three years as SPU's provost. Eaton has experience spanning both higher education and business. During a 17-year tenure, he held a variety of positions in the English department at Whitworth College (WA), including department chair and humanities division chair. In 1992-93 he served as Whitworth's interim president. Before his tenure at Whitworth, he was president of a family business.

Dr. Richard Hughes is distinguished professor of religion at Pepperdine University. He earned his Ph.D. from the University of Iowa and has taught at Abilene Christian University and Southwest Missouri State University. He was the co-director with William Adrian of the Lilly Endowment project examining the theological and historical roots of Christian higher education which produced the work *Models for Christian Higher Education*, co-edited with Adrian.

Dr. Robert Wuthnow is the senior fellow and director of the Center for the Study of Religion and Society at Princeton University. He is the author of numerous works including *Producing the Sacred*. Wuthnow is considered one of the leading authorities in the United States on the interaction of religion and American culture.

Dr. Timothy Beuthin is the director of Leadership Development for the Free Methodist Church of North America. He earned his Ph.D. from Michigan State University while serving as dean of students and faculty member at Spring Arbor College. He served as consulting editor for this book.

Foreword

As the cycle turns into a new millennium, one senses that the Christian college is moving toward a defining moment. Is its vision clear? Are its roots intact? Is its education different? Is its influence needed? These are the questions that must be addressed and answered if the Christian college continues to serve with vitality in the 21st century.

Defining moments are not few for the Christian college. In its long and distinguished history since the founding of Harvard College in 1640, the destiny of this institution has turned upon the challenge of change. Intellectual challenges, such as French deism in the 18th century, German empiricism in the 19th century, and American secularism in the 20th century, have led the way. Incompatible with the biblical roots upon which the institution was founded, defining moments have come when trustees, presidents and educational leaders have made the conscious choice of consistent theological and philosophical positions.

Many Christian colleges and universities experienced spiritual renewal at turning points in each of the past three centuries. Others continued on a path that took them farther away from their biblical roots and spiritual influence. More often than not, with this defection, they severed their ties with their founding denominations and declared themselves as independents.

Throughout the history of American higher education, Christian colleges and universities have also come periodically to defining moments brought on by financial exigency. The record shows that scores of schools founded in the latter decades of the 19th century no longer exist. Reasons for their demise may vary, but financial crisis is almost always the underlying factor. Even Christian colleges that have continued to exist since that time are not exempt from their own moments of financial brinkmanship. In the 1960s when public higher education was rising to its crest, for instance, some studies projected that two-thirds of private colleges, primarily in the Christian college sector, would either die or barely survive in the margins of academic quality due to shriveling financial resources.

Recent history has proven the prophets wrong. If financial exigency in the 1960s and 1970s brought Christian colleges to a defining moment, they turned the challenge into conquest. Rather than disappearing in droves or wallowing in mediocrity, Christian colleges and universities are celebrating their success, not just in enrollment growth and fiscal solvency, but in a significant role as major players in American higher education.

Success brings with it responsibility. Perhaps for the first time in its history, the Christian college or university has come to a defining moment created by the crisis of success rather than the crisis of faith or finances. With a strong position in the educational marketplace, recognition in the academic community, favor for government funding, acceptability by the profession and compatibility with the conservative subculture, the Christian college is not compelled to ask hard questions about its mission and its character. Instead, success makes it most vulnerable to the seductive sirens of a secular culture. Confrontations are minimal when a market mentality begins to drive the mission, function slips ahead of faith, tolerance eases out conviction, and efficiency overrides effectiveness. When it happens, the Christian college loses its distinguishing character — a curriculum centered in the liberal arts, an educational process dedicated to the integration of faith and learning, a campus climate conducive to spiritual formation, and social impact aimed at transformation in the church and the culture. Just the mention of these defining qualities is sufficient to remind us that some Christian colleges have already lost their distinctive edge. Like yellow flags flying in the wind, they serve as a warning for the whole sector.

One might argue in favor of success in the Christian college by saying,

"If it ain't broke, don't fix it." The wisdom of experienced leadership, however, contends, "If it ain't broke, it's time to fix it." This is the motive behind the writing of the book *The University Through the Eyes of Faith*. At the height of success of Christian higher education, Steve Moore has asked thoughtful observers of the contemporary scene to join him in reflecting upon the key issues confronting the faith-affirming college as it comes to another defining moment.

Imagine yourself in a room with a man who stops at the end of each day to sit in a chair facing a blank wall. In his mind's eye, he envisions the events of the day being rerun across the wall as if it were a motion picture screen. As he watches the scenes, he asks himself, "What do I see?" "What can I learn?" and "What must I do?"

A similar setting has been created for the authors of this book. Dr. Moore invited prominent university professors along with a college president and a university pastor to sit together before a blank wall and visualize the stream of historical events, theological tenets, learning processes, campus values and cultural relationships which portray the contemporary Christian college. After reflecting upon what they saw, the authors then framed the answers to the questions "What do we see?" "What can we learn?" and "What must we do?" Although the responses are diverse and not without occasional tension, there is the unity of the eye of faith through which the image of the university is seen.

Dare we see the future of the university through the eyes of faith? Critics will be quick to claim a bias which counters the freedom of independent inquiry. Houston Smith, renown as a philosopher at the Massachusetts Institute of Technology, would be equally quick to note that a confession of Christian faith is more intellectually honest than the bias of "hidden assumptions" that other scholars may refuse to admit. So, with the confidence that the eye of faith has intellectual credibility for seeing the learning process in a university setting, the authors are honest in criticism, humble in conclusions and hopeful in outlook. None of them creates the identity of the Christian college by bashing their counterparts in the public or secular setting. Rather, one senses that their message is aimed primarily at institutions for whom the clarification of their vision is essential to their identity.

Jesus Himself confirms the value of seeing through the eyes of faith when He says, "The eye is the lamp of the body." In simplest truth, He makes the eye the entry point for the soul and then goes on to declare that what the eye sees pervades the whole body and determines its quality. In the same sense, when the university is seen through the eye of faith, the vision infuses mind and spirit into every aspect of the educational experience and gives an unmistakable quality to campus life.

So, as the Christian college comes to another defining moment for the 21st century, we have an unusual opportunity to see its future through the eye of faith in this book. The invitation is open. As we read, let us ask, "What do we see?" "What can we learn?" and "What must we do?" Answers to these questions framed by the authors and filled in by their readers offer high hopes for higher learning as it comes to another defining moment.

In the spirit of this forum, let the conversation begin.

David L. McKenna

David McKenna, president of Asbury Theological Seminary from 1982-94, also served tenures as president of Spring Arbor College and Seattle Pacific University. He was named 1993 Outstanding Educator by Religious Heritage of America. He is the author of numerous books, including *Awake! My Conscience!*, *A Future with a History: The Wesleyan Witness of the Free Methodist Church* and several volumes of the *Communicator's Commentary*.

Acknowledgments

To attempt to acknowledge those who contribute to the crafting, thinking and work of a project is nearly as difficult as the project itself. It is a great exercise in humility and gratitude as one realizes how fortunate one is to have the gift of such remarkable friends and colleagues.

First a word of thanks to Carol Quinlan, Carla Bull and Janet Oberembt for their faithful typing, revising, suggesting, encouraging and patiently accepting one more round of my revisions.

A special thanks to Curtis Martin who first encouraged and supported me in the pursuit of this project. His constant reminder that "the Son of Man came not to be served but to serve" (Matthew 20:28) is an important theme for any and all who labor in ministry in higher education. David and Janet McKenna have been friends, mentors and models. I am deeply indebted to colleagues with whom I've worked — David LeShana, Sam Dunn, Marj Johnson, Don Mortenson, Bob McIntosh, Ken Leonard, Phil Eaton, Martin Abbott and Bruce Murphy — for grace given and lessons learned together.

For students who have contributed in enormous ways to my thinking, my spiritual formation and my family's life, I cannot begin to say thank you enough. Their humor, fresh perspectives, energy, creativity and surprises are a constant source of joy, encouragement and motivation. Centurions and Group guys — Jeff, Doug, Lloyd, Chris, Mark, Chris, Greg, Aaron, Josh, Nate, Brandon, Seth, Kaylan, Bruce, Mark, Brian and Chad — you are da' men. Thanks too to the members of the Southwest Leadership Foundation who are faithful sojourners.

For my colleagues in Campus Life, I am deeply grateful. They are educators with whom I've been blessed to serve and be about the business of Building Lives, often in the face of enormous challenges. They are as gifted, supportive and fun-loving a group of colleagues as can be found anyplace. Together they, with the remarkable group of faculty colleagues with whom we are blessed to work, make for a community of learners that is vibrant, thoughtful and engaging.

For the numerous individuals with whom I have been blessed to spend time in symposia, guest lectures, inauguration events and chapels, I am sincerely appreciative. They have sharpened my thinking, introduced me to new ideas, and inspired me to better work. Some are contributors to this volume and others, though their names don't appear, have contributed as well. I am particularly appreciative of the University of Illinois Press for the use of portions of Robert Wuthnow's work, and Euguene Peterson, whose writings and teachings have been a great influence on me. Chapter 1 draws in part on "Spirit and the Intellect on the University Campus," done in partnership with Dr. Peterson and which originally appeared in *Response.*

My wife Thanne, son Madison, and daughters Maegan and Mollie are the light of my life. They bring joy, laughter, energy and challenge to my world and soul. Thanks for being patient when I've been near deadlines and for the backrubs after long days and nights.

Finally, I want to thank Tim Beuthin for his special role of consulting editor. He understood the "message" and through suggestions and questions helped make this a better work. I am thankful to Tim and John Van Valin for sharing the vision, being willing to partner, and for working so hard to make this project happen.

Steve Moore

Education is not the filling of a pail, but the lighting of a fire.

—W.B. Yeats

INTRODUCTION
Is the Dream Alive?

Steve Moore

"Humans," writes Notre Dame philosopher Alasdair, "are essentially story-telling animals." And in saying this, he tells us what any young child already knows: Everyone likes a good story.

There are more than 800 church-related colleges and universities in the United States. And talking about great stories — the foundings of these institutions, many around 100 years ago, are full of stories of great faith, supreme sacrifice, tough times and colorful characters.

Though the stories of each institution are unique, a common theme prevails in almost every case ... a belief and commitment to a greater story. The belief was that the world was forever changed by the coming of Jesus Christ into the world. The commitment was that higher education could and should be Christian and that higher learning should shape and cultivate the lives of its students.

In almost every case, church-related colleges and universities were founded with the vision of serving the church and society. Higher education would be for both mind and spirit. The schools' commitment was evangelical, to spread the influence of the gospel; their commitment was practical, to provide trained leaders for the church and communities; and their commitment was social, to develop the talents that would prepare young men and women for lives of success and service.

Unfortunately, if many of those early founders could see their colleges and universities today they would be shocked, dismayed or perplexed. In far too many of these colleges and universities the story has taken strange twists and turns. The fire of Christian commitment that was the driving force of their founding and early growth has often been extinguished or severely dampened on far too many church-related college campuses.

The church, which was the "mother" of all these colleges and universities, is now held at arm's length or excluded altogether from any substantive involvement in the leadership and life of many of these institutions. With the exception of their willingness to accept students and dollars from the church, many church-related colleges have in fact become embarrassed about their Christian past.

Unfortunately, the story of how these and other institutions got to their current state is a complex one and not easily told. Financial viability, the influence of culture, the changing philosophical and ideological nature of the academy, and many more factors have combined to lead many institutions away from their roots. For some colleges and universities, these changes have led to the schools' demise. For others, the changes led them to become "independent" or "secular." But for many institutions, the good news is that their story is not yet finished.

Today many individuals and institutions are seeking to reclaim their heritage, refocus their mission, rethink their future and rededicate themselves to the task of Christian higher education. Opportunities abound for colleges and universities to rediscover and reassert those distinctives which make them unique in both their contribution to American higher education and their influence upon student lives.

What follows are some outstanding thinkers who, as leaders in higher education, are helping envision the future for Christian higher learning. Their wisdom and insights will be helpful to faculty, staff, administrators, trustees and other constituencies as they seek to make the vision a reality in the educational experiences of thousands of students around the world.

Fifty years ago, Pitirim Sorokin, founder of the sociology department at Harvard University, released a remarkable book, *The Crisis of Our Age*. In it, he predicted that our culture was on a course leading to self-destruction. He concluded with the stark offering of one hope — which stands as both a promise and challenge to our church and her colleges: *"Benedictus qui venit in nomine Domini* ... Blessed is the one who comes in the name of the Lord."

CHAPTER 1
The University as a Place of Spiritual Formation

Steve Moore

Begin with the Beginning in Mind

One cannot read John Elliot's declaration of 1643, "New England's First Fruits," and remain unmoved by the clarity and the commitment of the early settler's mission for higher learning in the "New World."

> After God had carried us safe to New England, and we had builded our houses, provided necessaries for our livelihood, rear'd convenient places for God's worship, and settled the civil government: One of the next things we longed for, and looked after, was to advance learning and perpetuate it to posterity, dreading to leave an illiterate ministry to the churches, when our present ministers shall lie in the durt.[1]

Elliot and this band of "New World" Christians shared an "Old World" dream where a learned clergy gave moral, spiritual and intellectual leadership to the community. Their wisdom was also informed by a particular experience in higher learning. No fewer than 34 of the early settlers, including one named "John Harvard," had roots in England's Emmanuel College of Cambridge University. The school that those early settlers would found, and which would bear John Harvard's name, was to become the first of more than 3,000 institutions that we have today dedicated to higher learning in America. From that founding of Harvard until the Civil War, most American colleges were founded by the church. This was not unique or surprising as the church had given birth to higher learning at every stage in the Western world for hundreds of years prior.

As the new nation grew, so grew the number of colleges that the church would start to serve the growing populace. As the fledgling democracy grew and industrialization took hold, the curriculum was soon broadened to include education and training for other professions along with the standard "training for ministry" which had been the primary focus of those earlier days. By the mid-1800s "state" colleges were added to the "pool" of American higher education, further broadening the access to education and further expanding the curriculum.

Even in this growth mode during the first two centuries, American educators remained clear on their central task and primary responsibility: the building of students' character. This shaping of students' character was not mere nebulous, moral instruction; it was clearly understood as Christian formation. Matters of faith and doctrine, as well as conduct and lifestyle, were of concern to educators and a responsibility assumed by the educational institutions at all levels.

However, as the dawning of a new era emerged with the coming of the 20th century, so the mission of higher education began to change dramatically. The reasons for these changes are complex. The result of these changes was widespread, from public to private institutions, from primary to graduate education. Historian George Marsden describes these changes. They came about as the result of three major forces in American culture:

1) those having to do with scientific and technological advances,

2) those having to do with ideological conflicts, and

3) those having to do with the growing religious and cultural pluralism.[2]

While understanding these forces of change is critical to understanding both the nature of American colleges and universities and its current state, the purpose of this essay takes us in a different direction. Many now see that while gains have been made and progress achieved in the growth and maturing of American higher education, some important things have been lost.

Our task is to once again raise the question which has repeatedly surfaced throughout higher education's history: Can and should the university be a place of spiritual formation? Across the centuries of education in Western civilization, the concern was for the whole person and for the student's intellectual, spiritual and social development. Why not now?

In the Greek academies, Talmudic schools, medieval universities and until the turn of the 20th century, the question was not "if" but when, where and how the intellect and character could be cultivated in the educational experience. In that context we can see that the experience of higher learning in the 20th century is an anomaly to the history of higher learning. As philosopher Alasdair MacIntyre states:

> Our moral premises are like so many incommensurable fragments of lost languages. The value concepts we use, deprived of the contexts in which they formerly made sense, have become mere means of expressing our feelings and manipulating others. Where once there was coherent discourse on the virtues and the common good, we now have the assertion of Nietzschean wills, marked by moral fictions, managed by bureaucrats ... The barbarians are not waiting beyond the frontiers, they have already been governing us for quite some time. And it is our lack of consciousness of this that constitutes part of our predicament.[3]

And so as we mark the turn of another century, we are challenged to ask "education for what purpose, learning for what end?"

It Is Not What We Thought It Would Be

To read most college catalogs, one would think that character formation was still at the heart of every institution in America. Eloquent prose about "shaping values," "integrating ethics," "leading productive lives," and "being liberally educated" fills the pages. However, those "close up" to the work of colleges and universities confess that there is remarkable uncertainty about the impact of the educational experience. As one faculty member jokingly remarked, "The one thing we can say for sure is that we keep most students out of their parents' hair and away from the workplace for at least four more years of growing up. ..." Or on a more serious reflective note, a college president observed, "I think the reason [colleges and universities] have been resistant to [outcomes assessment] is our fear that we will discover that we have little if any impact upon our students' lives. We are afraid the emperor will be shown to have no clothes."

For many a board member, the introduction to the world of Christian higher education is like being set down in a foreign country. The language, culture, customs and taboos of the academy seem complex and overwhelming. *It seemed like such a normal place*, they think to themselves. *How do they ever get anything done?* Worries about finances, lawsuits, enrollment and accreditation hardly give one time to think about the spiritual purposes of an institution. "If we can just get more faculty to go to chapel and more students to stay awake in chapel … then hopefully it will do someone some good. …"

For many new faculty members the introduction to the world of higher education as a professor is like a jolt to the system. No one in graduate school talked about committees, pension plans, faculty senate or advising hordes of people who have not decided what to do with their lives. "Where is the time for my research, for writing, for thinking? How can I possibly be concerned with a student's spiritual life when I have yet to answer some of my own questions?" Educational staff can also be surprised by the reality of campus life. Eager to contribute to building a vital campus culture and rich cocurricular experience for students, staff are sometimes marginalized as "party planners" or caricatured as anti-intellectual.

Then there is the student. After the shock of university life has worn off, it is not unusual for one reality about Christian higher education to become painfully clear for new students: It is no "Sunday school" experience. Christian students commonly enter college motivated by a commitment to God and a desire to serve their Lord. Then they find themselves either distracted or deflected from that intention at every turn. They find themselves immersed in rigorous academics. They find themselves staying up late at night reading Foucault or Camus. They wake up in the morning puzzled over questions they never knew existed.

This is not what they had bargained on. Their professors seem far more interested in their spelling than their spirituality. They find themselves spending far more time on paradigms than in prayer. What many hope to be the collecting of proofs to buttress their faith is instead a testing by fire.

Many students do not come to school with a good understanding of what they are getting into. In addition to admonitions about getting enough sleep and eating right, more than a few have been warned of the dangers of higher education. Though most parents, pastors and friends support higher education, a certain nervousness is also present as the student goes to school. This nervousness isn't helped by the fact that more than a few Christian groups or traditions have little use for "higher education."

"Thinking about God gets you into nothing but trouble," they suggest. "Don't let them fill your head with questions and doubt."

Or "the wisdom of man is foolishness in the eyes of God."

"Only praise and believe" are the words of counsel offered to many university-bound students. "After all," they might continue, "universities, in general, and religion and philosophy departments in particular are 'known' to be graveyards of spirituality and the place where men and women are likely to lose their faith."[4]

While some students might get lectures on "safe sex" or "alcohol awareness," Christian students are likely to get a "safe faith" sermon from some well-intentioned soul. The message of the sermon is this: The brain, if used to carry out basic everyday functions (like reading the comics or checking the box scores), is considered fairly harmless. But if you presume to think about God and His ways, about the injustices in our world, or the incongruities in what is known, you are likely to get into trouble. To ask hard questions of sacred things, and to read big books by people of no faith, is likely to produce a mental malignancy that will spread rapidly to your soul.

Though a bit of that "sermon" might be overstated, we cringe in part because we know it contains an element of truth. We all know people who, for a variety of reasons, abandoned their faith in their university years. By and large, the university has not been a congenial place in which to nurture a life of prayer, a community of love and a risky faith. Ever since the Age of Enlightenment, which encouraged the split between the heart (faith) and head (reason), schools have not been easy allies in a life of worship, witness or the love of God. Talking about God can easily become the antithesis of talking to God. Even though the same words are used in our talking, they are not the same thing at all.[5]

If one gets the impression that the university is not a particularly congenial place for spiritual formation, then it must be quickly noted that neither is any other "place." Whether it is the church, home, mountaintop, monastery or golf course, "place" has not been the defining characteristic to identify where God is at work.

People, not places, tend to be better indicators of where God is at work. And the good news is that God is at work in men and women in colleges and universities, and some of them happen to be professors, staff, coaches, students and even presidents and trustees! These institutions of higher learning have no more and no less of their share of conflicts, feuds and problems than any other place where Christians live and do their work. So, if a Christian college itself is not holy ground, at least it doesn't discourage bushes from bursting into flame from time to time. And, when a bush does burst into flame, it helps to have people around who might know what it is and, more importantly, what our response should be.

Therefore, the first and most important lesson to learn about spiritual formation, it seems, is that it is not primarily a function of place or curricula. This was a hard lesson for the people of Israel to learn, even when they had God regularly reminding them of that in ways one would think would get their attention. So we should not be surprised that it may take us a while to recognize this rather simple and obvious lesson. But once we do, we can quit expecting either books, people or institutions to provide for that which is already sitting in our backyard. From the moment of that recognition, we are freed from a lot of grumbling and complaining in the wilderness. Places and people are also freed from unreal expectations of being either security or saviors and instead become companions on a journey.[6]

While the Christian university does not provide all of the materials necessary for spiritual formation, it can provide conditions, valuable resources and experienced companions through which formation can take place for a relatively brief yet strategic period of time in a student's life.

The university's condition is also one characterized by words — words spoken, words written, words read. Books, containers for words, are everywhere. Classrooms, designed for the audition of words, are the primary architecture. Computers, a technology for the recording and retrieval of words, are ubiquitous. The university is a world of words.

Recognizing this is essential in dealing with matters of spiritual formation in the university. When we ask the question, "What can we do to make the university a better place for spiritual formation?" we must also ask, "How can we enter into and embrace the unique condition that constitutes the campus in such a way that we grow up into maturity of Christ Jesus?" "How can we bridge the chasm between God's Word and our words and lives?" "How can we encourage the Word to become flesh in our lives and the lives of our students?" These are important questions to which first-rate Christian minds have given considerable attention in every century of the church's existence.

In every generation this struggle — how to keep the mind and heart of faith connected — has been a familiar one. As John Wesley so aptly reminds us, "A man [sic] may be orthodox in every point, he may not only espouse right opinions but zealously defend them against all opposers ... and still not be authentically religious [Christian]."[7] Just as the mind can be disconnected from the heart of faith, so can the heart be disconnected from the mind of faith. This, unfortunately, is more characteristic of contemporary Christianity where faith is presented as feelings and experience, able to fulfill psychological needs and disconnected from transforming, timeless truths.

The challenge to "unite the two so oft divided — vital piety and sound learning" has continued to be present with us. Fortunately God has and will continue to call men and women to lives of thought, prayer and the work of bringing these two together. Some of these are well-known individuals like Augustine, Aquinas, Pascal, Luther, Calvin or Wesley. Others are not so familiar to the 20th-century Christian, but we have much to learn from them.

One unfamiliar but extraordinarily helpful approach to the subject of spiritual formation comes to us from the unlikely place of the Egyptian desert. It was there that Evagrius Ponticus, sometimes known as Evagrius the Solitary, spent nearly 20 years nurturing a life of thought and prayer. From 380 A.D. until his death in 399 A.D., he wrote about matters of intellect and prayer with the clarity and wisdom that make him such a good guide for us today.

The thought, said Evagrius, that is inattentive, unresponsive or indifferent to God's Word, no matter what its content (and actual contents could be very good indeed), becomes a diversion from God or even an actual defiance of God. The goal, the highest good of the human creature, is that knowledge of God and prayer to God converge. Knowledge that does not lead to or become prayer to God is, in Evagrius' analysis, demonic — a spirituality divorced from obedience to God.[8]

It is a simple distinction, which, with a little practice, we can learn to make for ourselves. The university is as good a place as any to begin making these distinctions. In fact, it is probably the very best place to begin doing it, for there is hardly an hour in a day when there is not an occasion in which to exercise these fundamental discernments.

The French have a wonderful phrase, *deformation professionale*, to refer to maladies we are particularly liable to in the course of pursuing our line of work. Physicians are in constant danger of becoming callused to suffering, lawyers are in danger of cynicism about justice, and those of us who study and work in Christian higher education are in danger of having the very words we use about God separate us from God, the most damning deformation of all.[9]

Such a warning echoes the caution of the Apostle Paul when he admonished us not to be deceived by the "wisdom of the world." But there is not a hint of anti-intellectualism in that or any other teaching of Paul. Again and again he reminds us of the importance of being thinking, not just feeling, Christians when he says to "take every thought captive to obey Christ," "have the mind of Christ" and "be transformed by the renewing of your mind."[10] But Paul also knows that thought, even when it is about God (maybe even especially when it is about God) can all too easily become self-serving, prideful and (using Evagrius' bold designation) demonic — if it is not brought vigorously, regularly and devoutly before the living God in prayerful obedience. This cannot happen in individual isolation. It happens best in community. It is most effectively accomplished in the midst of a university community that worships, plays, studies, questions, argues and encourages one another in the practice of allowing the Word to become flesh in our lives.

But there is also a sense in which the university cannot do this for itself. It requires a larger community of faith. It requires men and women, scattered throughout our culture and our world, seeking to "take every thought captive unto Christ" and seeking to challenge one another to do so in all we do. As St. Francis so ably reminds us, "Preach the Gospel in everything you do and, if necessary, use words." Perhaps an occasional "capture that thought" scrawled on a classroom wall wouldn't be a bad idea either.

ENDNOTES

1. J. Winthrop, *History of New England* (New York: Scribners Press, 1908).
2. George M. Marsden, *The Soul of the American University* (New York: Oxford University Press, 1994).
3. Alasdair MacIntyre, *After Virtue* (Notre Dame: Notre Dame Press, 1984).
4. Eugene Peterson with Steve Moore, "Spirit and Intellect on the University Campus," *Response* (March, 1994).
5. Ibid.
6. Ibid.
7. John Wesley, *Wesley's 52 Standard Sermons.* Ed., N. Burwash (Salem, Ohio: Schmul Publishers, 1967).
8. Eugene Peterson with Steve Moore, "Spirit and Intellect on the University Campus," *Response* (March, 1994).
9. Ibid.
10. Holy Bible, *Revised Standard Version,* 1 Corinthians 3:19; 2 Corinthians 10:5; 1 Corinthians 2:16; Romans 12:2 (Nashville: Thomas Nelson Inc., 1971).

CHAPTER 2
Christian Education: A Generational Retrospective

William E. Hull

The road to tomorrow, more often than not, leads through yesterday. Only when we remember whence we have come are we able to assess whither we should go. That is why it is important that we take a look back over the past half century when Christian higher education emerged as a national force and became a significant player in the field of higher education.[1] As the founders of that era move off the scene, new leaders search for the sources of resiliency and adaptability that have brought us to this point. What are the burdens and the blessings of the legacy from those tumultuous decades?

The Beginning of a New Era

The year 1946 is a useful point at which to launch our retrospective, since it marks the beginning of a new era in American higher education as well as the birth of the modern evangelical movement. After wartime years when civilian enrollments plummeted and college finances were precarious, veterans suddenly began to crowd every campus, over a million of them in the first year, 1946. The so-called GI Bill[2] which financed this peacetime invasion represented the most important federal policy initiative since the Morrill Act of 1862. Coupled with the federal funding of military research during World War II, it marked the entry of national government into post-secondary education as a major player to this day. Most important for our purposes, it decisively tilted the dominant force in academia from the private to the public sector. As late as 1951, a majority of students were still enrolled in private institutions, whereas since then enrollments in public institutions have steadily grown until they now stand at 79 percent.[3] It is not that the GI Bill favored public institutions over private but that the public purse provided the only source of funding massive enough to respond to the hunger for universal access which the bill stimulated. Some even wondered aloud if the private colleges of the 20th century would go the way of the private academies of the 19th century, which virtually disappeared after public secondary education became universally available.

Once the politicians learned from this venture just how helpful higher education could be as an instrument of national policy, they became even more aggressive in offering federal funding, especially after the Sputnik crisis of 1957 suggested that we might be lagging behind the Russians in technology. Suddenly vast sums of money were legislated, not only to "catch up" scientifically with our enemies, but also to bring higher education into the "Great Society" of Lyndon B. Johnson.[4] Dazzled by this plenitude of federal largesse, many Christian educators were tempted to depict their institutions as "secular" in order to qualify for urgently needed funds. The language of the legislation, which shaped the qualifying criteria, pressured schools to limit the religious dimension on campus to one organization, meeting at one place, with no real involvement in academic life. The issue was vigorously debated by church bodies without coming to any consensus except that the pervasiveness of government involvement was both inevitable and inimical to the fostering of Christian distinctives.

The most ominous thing about federal intervention in the private sector was not that government was inherently anti-intellectual or even anti-religious, but that it represented the political expression of a culture that was becoming increasingly secular through the '60s and '70s as the superficial religious revival of the '50s ran its course. Educators were no more exempt than politicians from this revolt, which threatened to sweep everything before it. Beginning with the free speech movement at Berkeley in 1964, and continuing until the abdication of President Richard M. Nixon in 1974, student unrest began to erupt with increasing militancy until some of our most distinguished universities found themselves engulfed in conflict. As rationality proved helpless to resolve angry grievances, as veteran educators were locked in or out of their offices according to the whims of student radicals, as college presidents resigned in droves, a siege mentality settled over many campuses and chastened academicians began to talk openly about a collapse of values and a crisis of purpose.

Even as education was enduring its nightmare of the "Death of Reason," religion was enduring its nightmare of the "Death of God." In the mainline denominations, which had invested so much in the "Christian University Movement" between 1920 and 1960,[5] the emphasis quickly shifted from a concern for the Christian mission of the university in the modern world to the purely internal concerns of the university for new modes of learning and for interdisciplinary studies. The strategy of developing a Christian intellectual leadership which would function from within the university to influence its basic direction was replaced by a strategy of affirming the autonomy of the university as "a secular institution operating by its own canons."[6] Instead of advocating Christianity with the same passion that an English professor might advocate Shakespeare or an art professor might advocate Rembrandt,[7] most academic representatives of religion sought instead "the establishment of legitimacy in the arts and sciences through the development of a posture of analytical rigor, of disinterested objectivity, and sometimes of disinterested irreverence."[8]

In reviewing the literature of the turbulent '60s, it is striking to observe that the university itself did not demand all of these capitulations as the price of honest dialogue with religion. Rather, one gains the impression that, faced with a precipitous decline in spiritual vitality on the one hand,[9] and the allure of life in "The Secular City" on the other,[10] many Christian intellectuals decided that there was more opportunity for career fulfillment — indeed, for vocational survival! — in joining a triumphalistic "Academic Revolution" already under way[11] than in defending an embattled Christianity whose obituary was being published on every hand. In any case, the collapse of the "Christian University Movement" was swift and complete.[12] By the time Claude Welch issued his programmatic essay on religion in higher education (1971), it was as if the whole epoch had never even existed.[13]

As the academic study of religion became increasingly secularized by deliberate design rather than by unconscious drift and as this approach, in the first flush of its popularity on secular campuses, sought to consolidate its gains by denigrating confessional approaches to the study of religion, churchmen who had long advocated a partnership approach to higher education began to have second thoughts. Some "church-related" schools came to be viewed with increasing suspicion, funding levels were eroded, a few were allowed to close, and talk was openly heard in denominational circles about "cutting ties" which had endured, in many cases, for more than a century. On the whole, there was a noticeable drop in enthusiasm for Christian higher education in "Old-Line Protestantism" during the '60s and '70s which provided an opportunity for evangelical schools to increase their influence.[14]

Although campus turmoil led to some useful educational reforms on the school side, the most sinister thing it did on the church side was to help arouse a dormant fundamentalism which proved to be the most potent religious force in the '80s. After its heyday in the mid-'20s, fundamentalism was badly discredited and driven to the fringes of American cultural and religious life where it remained a marginal influence for a half century (1930-80).[15] But when the universities themselves became hotbeds of rioting, drug culture and sexual promiscuity — as well as the source of that technological pragmatism which gave us Vietnam! — then fundamentalism found its chance to come roaring back into the fray. Capitalizing on a campus chaos that seemed to presage the collapse of the "modernity" culture long championed by secular education, neofundamentalism quickly gained social legitmization with the ascendancy of Ronald Reagan to the U.S. presidency and exploited this newfound status to become a powerful influence on mainstream American religious and political life.[16]

Although this New Right Religion was "new" in the sophistication with which it exploited the electronic media, it was unfortunately "old" in the fateful baggage of anti-intellectualism it carried from a more distant past.[17] The evidence is all about us: the ill-conceived effort to mandate the teaching of "scientific creationism," as if such legislation could somehow destroy the demon of "Darwinism,"[18] the militant campaign against "secular humanism" which reflected little understanding of what either "secularity" or "humanism" really means;[19] and the simplistic use of "conservatism" and "liberalism" as labels for "true" and "false" in ways that would baffle Edmund Burke and John Locke alike.[20] And yet this dogmatic absolutism continues to flourish rather than wither, even among faculty and students, because many who oppose it have nothing better to offer than a narcissistic subjectivity of self-fulfilling "experience."[21]

Looking now at both sides of the religion/education dialogue in American life, we find any possibility of a partnership in shambles. From the school side, even some who work most directly with religion seem mortally afraid to assert its value-claims over the life of their institutions. From the church side, those in leadership positions seem determined to distance themselves even from the modest intellectual gains made by the Christian faith over decades of painful struggle. There is simply no middle ground! Both partners have renounced the dialogue and either dug in to fight or turned to intramural concerns that ignore the other's existence. What are we to do about this angry confrontation, this "dialogue of the deaf" where neither side can even hear what the other is saying? That may well be the most momentous question now facing those with a serious concern for Christian higher education in the evangelical tradition.

Three Challenges Inherited in the Last 50 Years

Our swift survey of the past half century has identified an interlocking cluster of intractable issues with which every leader in Christian higher education has been forced to struggle. In light of this history, let me now attempt to summarize three of the challenges bequeathed to us by the last 50 years.

[1] There was a time when both school and church drew their understanding of reality and their sense of legitimacy from the same cultural tributaries, but this is less and less the case today. When ideological underpinnings diverge, different value systems are constructed which make it difficult to achieve congruity of expectations. Frustrations multiply because the two partners do not seem to share the same sense of mission. Feeding this discontent is the suspicion that the two entities are constructing their sense of identity from different if not incompatible sources.

Much evangelical church life today has left behind those sturdier Reformation and Puritan roots that came to flower in John Wesley and Jonathan Edwards, building instead upon the revivalism, fundamentalism and pietism of the late 19th and early 20th centuries. One of its finest historians, Mark Noll, has brilliantly analyzed the devastating intellectual consequences of this triadic union. "The combination of 'victorious-living' Holiness and premillennial dispensationalism was, for the promotion of Christian thinking, an absolute disaster. It was a disaster because the supernaturalism of dispensationalism ... was gnostic ... [it] pushed analysis away from the visible present to the invisible future."[22] Again: "Evangelicals who think that the basic intellectual operations performed by the modern research universities can be conceded to 'the world' without doing fundamental damage to the cause of Christ may think of themselves as orthodox Christians. In reality, however, they are modern-day Manichaeans, gnostics, or docetists."[23]

In the academy meanwhile, there is a tenacious clinging to the Enlightenment paradigm of Cartesian objectivity, partly because it is feared that a postmodern paradigm might lead to the escapist subjectivity that Noll decries. Even when academicians such as Page Smith show the sterility of Enlightenment thinking,[24] scholars who control the graduate school culture through which every Ph.D. candidate must pass refuse to embrace a post-Enlightenment epistemology, which might take more seriously the spiritual dimensions of human experience. They are afraid that it will not preserve the hard-won scientific gains of the last four centuries. What this means, among other things, is that virtually all entry-level faculty members in our evangelical schools bring with them an intellectual *Weltanschauung* hopelessly at odds with the mindset in many of the supporting churches, a clash of presuppositions that both parties are woefully unprepared to resolve.

[2] Because church and school are fed by different cultural tributaries, it is not surprising that they adopt contrasting strategic stances. I have found the familiar categories developed by H. Richard Niebuhr helpful in analyzing this tension.[25] From the church side, the combination of revivalism, fundamentalism and pietism fosters a "Christ *against* culture" approach, what Ernst Troeltsch might call a "sectarian" strategy. The overriding desire is to offer an alternative culture and lifestyle to those reacting against the deepening crisis in Western civilization with its loss of meaning, lack of norms, rampant hedonism, moral malaise, rise of violence, breakdown of the family, and cheapening of the sanctity of life. Nor is it hard to include a rejection of higher education in this indictment, granted the torrent of recent criticism that has poured forth from some of its own leaders.

By contrast, almost all of the pressure on Christian colleges and universities is to adopt a "Christ *in* culture" posture: inclusive rather than separatist, multicultural rather than homogeneous, mainstream rather than marginalized. Almost every day someone tries to define additional external obligations for the academy: to multiple accrediting agencies, to a host of regulatory bodies, and now to state and federal educational bureaucracies. The kind of academic reform urged by the educational establishment brings with it the requirement of accommodating ever greater diversity of both students and faculty. At the very moment when churches are trying to become more niche-oriented, more ideologically pure, and more culturally monolithic, those schools emphasizing Christian distinctiveness are under enormous pressure to move in the opposite direction.

Lurking under the surface here is a subtle difference of mood, of attitude, of atmosphere in which each entity does its work. As is often true of the "Christ against culture" posture, many churches reflect a growing pessimism compounded of several factors. A great many older congregations are located in areas where the population has been stagnant for years, and the prospects for growth are bleak indeed. Laboring in these circumstances produces a high level of leadership stress: ministerial burnout, forced terminations, frequent job turnover, working conditions that are austere at best. On top of this, in many denominations, is the persistence of controversy, fratricidal conflicts that inflict damage on all sides of the family to the apparent benefit of none.

By contrast, the colleges and universities tend to be located in flourishing areas that provide reasonable incentives for growth. There is relatively little upheaval in administrative or faculty leadership as compared with pastoral turnover in the churches. In a time of flat or declining contributions from religious sources, many schools have been able to attract ever more support elsewhere. While it would hardly be accurate to describe these campuses as havens of affluence, at least working conditions have steadily improved in recent decades. By and large, evangelical higher education in the past half century has been a success story. Enrollments grow, facilities expand, budgets enlarge, influence increases — and the result is a prevailing mood of optimism, of confidence in the future, of seeing progress that is likely to continue. While generalizations are risky when referring to such a complex situation, my daily experience is one of mediating between a pessimism in the churches that feeds defensiveness and frustration, and an optimism in the schools that feeds aggressiveness and self-confidence. Needless to say, the strategic consequences of these attitudinal differences are enormous.

[3] We need now to probe more deeply the implications of the disparate success rates in churches and schools. Since the early '60s ushered in a new era in American life, let us seek a generational perspective by comparing 1961 with 1991 in a case study of my own denomination, the Southern Baptist Convention. We may limit our inquiry here to one of the most

cherished indicators of success, financial growth. In 1961, the churches received $501,301,714 which grew to $4,704,986,720 in 1991, a gain of $4,203,685,006, or 838.6 percent. The schools, on the other hand, received $57,232,071 in 1961, which increased to $866,207,007 in 1991, a gain of $808,974,936, or 1,413.5 percent. This means that, over the last 30 years, Southern Baptist educational institutions have grown almost twice as fast as the churches that support them. It should come as no surprise, therefore, to learn that the rate of support for our denominational schools by the churches has steadily declined. In 1961, the various state conventions contributed $15,677,189 to their colleges and universities for operations and capital needs, which was 27.4 percent of income received. By 1991, the state conventions' contribution had increased to $91,140,639, but this was only 10.5 percent of income received. In other words, denominational support for Christian higher education today is little more than a third of what it was 30 years ago when measured by the total income of the institutions involved. For Southern Baptists to have given the same proportionate support to their schools in 1991 as they did in 1961 would have required a denominational contribution of $237,340,719, which is $146,200,080 more than they actually gave!

Two conclusions are obvious from the data. First, our educational institutions have been forced to find a rapidly increasing percentage of their support from non-denominational sources in order to sustain their present rate of growth. This is not so much a matter of deliberate "distancing" as it is a matter of fiscal survival!

Second, not only do our denominational agencies lack the funds to keep pace with the dynamic expansion of our schools, but they urgently need to divert even some of their reduced allocations for Christian higher education to more pressing needs in the face of flat or declining revenues from the churches when adjusted for inflation. Again, this may be not so much a sign of waning commitment to our educational institutions as it is a prioritizing of mission programs deemed essential to the ongoing growth and vitality of the denomination itself.

Evangelic Higher Education Over the Past 50 Years

In the face of these daunting difficulties, how has evangelical higher education fared over the past 50 years? Clearly the "governmentalizing" of the educational enterprise, the "secularizing" of the surrounding culture, and the "fundamentalizing" of the supporting churches have posed a supreme challenge to our educational leadership. This crisis in church-related schools was recognized in our generation's definitive exposition of American higher education, *The Academic Revolution* by Christopher Jencks and David Riesman.

Writing in 1968, the high-water mark of the difficulties traced above, our authors pointed out that 80 percent of the church colleges founded before 1865 were defunct by 1929 and concluded that the rest would soon follow suit:

> ... caught in a financial squeeze ... enrollment lagging behind ... competitive position will deteriorate." Their prediction: "The survival of recognizably Protestant colleges therefore seems to depend on the survival within the larger society of Protestant enclaves whose members believe passionately in a way of life radically different from that of the majority ...[26]

For "the holdouts" who refuse to join their "revolution," Jencks and Riesman offered this elegy:

> What then will become of the Protestant colleges? Some will doubtless become nonsectarian and absorb the overflow of students looking for brand-name labels. Others will probably be driven to the wall and after much soul-searching will try to sell themselves to the state. A few may combine with other neighboring institutions, and a few others will doubtless close their doors. But the great majority will probably struggle on, just as they have for a century or more. Lacking the resources to build a clientele on the basis of academic distinction, the location to build it on the basis of physical convenience, the connections to build it on the basis of social snobbery, and the competence

to build it on the basis of professional training, they will cling to their religious labels in order to escape complete anonymity.[27]

How does that condescending obituary uttered from the heights of Harvard look more than a quarter-century later? Contrary to estimates that as many as one-third of the denominational schools would be forced to close for financial reasons, virtually none have shut their doors even in a volatile economy that has reduced huge business corporations to ruin. Again, a case study from the Southern Baptist Convention with which I am most familiar: In 1966-67 when Jencks and Riesman wrote, Southern Baptists had 39 senior colleges and universities with 78,226 students. In 1993, they had 53 senior colleges and universities with 207,978 students. What about physical and financial resources? In 1966-67, these schools had property valued at $301,251,798 and endowments of $119,677,712, for a total of $420,929,510. By 1993, property was valued at $1,576,239,266 and endowments at $1,869,510,9489, for a total of $3,445,750,214.[28]

Finally, what about reputation? In all of the recent rankings of America's best colleges and universities, Southern Baptist institutions are prominently included for academic distinction, character-building and "best-buy" affordability, hardly fulfilling the predictions of Jencks and Riesman that they would just "struggle on"!

If we ask why (in the face of such formidable difficulties) evangelical colleges and universities have been able not only to survive, but also to flourish in this half century, one of the most objective answers I have found comes from outside our ranks, appropriately enough from the social historian Page Smith. In a passionate jeremiad of 1990 entitled *Killing the Spirit: Higher Education in America*, Smith goes back 50 years and more to explain evangelical success in these words:

> The small liberal-arts colleges, most of them denominational in their origins and still clinging to many of the ideals of a classical education, honored teaching above research and encouraged close relations between students and teachers. It was in such obscure and modest institutions that students received the

stimulus and encouragement to continue their studies at universities. A strange anomaly thus developed. While the universities had, in the main, a condescending attitude toward the small 'liberal-arts' colleges scattered throughout the hinterland, they clearly depended on them for a disproportionate number of their ablest graduate students.[29]

For example, as R.H. Knapp and H.B. Goodrich discovered in their *Origins of American Scientists*, "The colleges that produced the highest proportion of scientists were virtually all 'founded by Protestant denominations for the training of ministers and teachers.'"[30]

But why did the Christian colleges have a much higher "productivity index" that made them the "farm system" of the "great universities"?[31] Expanding on the conclusion of Knapp and Goodrich that their graduates possessed "certain distinguishing attributes of character" ... rooted in "fundamental Protestant virtues," Smith writes:

> The thousands (including those that fell by the wayside) of small denominational colleges across the country performed, in the aggregate, a critically important service to the nation. However bleak and austere many of them doubtless were, however limited in intellectual range and aesthetic sensibilities, the young men and women that they turned out decade after decade were individuals with, as we say today, strong internalized values ... men and women confident of their ability to remake the world, starting with the United States. They were the radicals, the reformers, the Populist politicians, state legislators, the enemies of the ... exploiters. They were the friends of the free black and the Indians, the champions of women's rights, the laborers for Christ in foreign lands as well as in 'domestic missions' among the urban poor and the newly arrived immigrants.[32]

What conclusions may be drawn from this "retrospective" of the last half century? First, our church-related schools may be small but they are tough. The forces that kill most kinds of institutions seem unable to deal them a death blow, which suggests that they serve deep human needs that are not easily denied. Second, the fittest endure because they know how to adapt. Faced with potentially fatal competition and drastically altered circumstances, they have relocated to new campuses, offered new programs, cultivated new constituencies, attracted new resources, and pursued new strategies. Third, these schools, as a group, have refused to absolutize either reason or faith as the only route to the apprehension of reality but have insisted that mind and heart alike must be cultivated if we are to grasp the fullness of what it means to be human. In refusing to fall into the epistemological trap posed by the Enlightenment, Christian higher education is positioned to make an even finer contribution in the next 50 years than it has in the last 50 years as it addresses the postmodern agenda of the 21st century.

ENDNOTES

1. For representative surveys of evangelicalism in American life since World War II see George Marsden, editor, *Evangelicalism and Modern America* (Grand Rapids: William B. Eerdmans, 1984).

2. This veterans' educational assistance act, Public Law 346, passed in June 1944, provided training for all military personnel who had served a minimum of 90 days in the armed forces.

3. It is instructive to study public vs. private enrollments from 1947 through 1992 as set forth in *Digest of Education Statistics 1994* (Washington: U.S. Department of Education, 1994), 176, Table 169. Statistics for 1995 are taken from *The Almanac of Higher Education 1995* (Chicago: University of Chicago Press, 1995), 4. It reports enrollments of 11,387,725 in public and 3,103,501 in private colleges and universities.

4. Key legislation was embodied in the National Defense Education Act of 1958 and the Higher Education Act of 1965. Large sums were made available for fellowships and assistantships, training grants and work-study opportunities. In the decade 1963-72, federal support of basic research increased from $610,000,000 to $1,409,000,000.

5. I have sought to tell this story in "Christian Higher Education at the Crossroads," *Perspectives in Religious Studies* 19 (1992): 441-454. For a much fuller treatment from a theological perspective see Douglas Sloan, *Faith and Knowledge: Mainline Protestantism and American Higher Education* (Louisville: Westminster John Knox, 1994).

6. Hubert C. Nobel, "Of Wine and Wineskins," *The Christian Scholar* 48 (Summer 1965): 170.

7. Ellen K. Coughlin, "The Ironic Detachment of Religion Scholars," *The Chronicle of Higher Education* (December 2, 1981: 20) quotes Robert McAfee Brown at a symposium on religion and the intellectual world: "In what strikes me as a strange irony, there is a passionate refusal to grant passion a place in the educational venture, an engaged insistence that disengagement is the only appropriate posture, and a partisan decision that partisanship has no place in the classroom."

8. James M. Gustafson, "The Study of Religion in Colleges and Universities: A Practical Commentary," *The Study of Religion in Colleges and Universities*, edited by Paul Ramsey and John F. Wilson (Princeton: Princeton University Press, 1970), 335.

9. In the academic world, this was symbolized by the momentary popularity of "Death of God" theology, which reached a media climax in the Easter cover story, "Toward a Hidden God," *Time*, 8 April 1966, 82-87. For the substance of this effort to plumb the ultimate depths of secularity, see the writings of Gabriel Vahanian, William Hamilton, Thomas J.J. Altizer and Paul M. Van Buren.

10. The allusion is to Harvey Cox, *The Secular City* (New York: Macmillan, 1965). In that work, Cox dismissed as mere "medievalism" the effort of the church to establish its own schools and insisted that the idea of developing "Christian universities" in America was theologically bankrupt even before it began. Chided by his critics for dismissing as catastrophic every effort of the churches to relate to the universities, Cox revised his chapter on the university "to make clear that it is not the organized church as such that is unwelcome in the university, but its institution-centered and imperialist attitude" ("Preface to the Revised Edition," *The Secular City* [New York: Macmillan, 1966], xii). Apparently it did not occur to Cox that universities are also capable of an "institution-centered and imperialist attitude" that would plunge them into profound grief in the very period when he was writing! There is not space here to elucidate the enormous irony of Cox's later book, *Religion in the Secular City* (New York: Simon and Schuster, 1984), which not only announces the impending collapse of that Western bourgeois "modernism" on which so many universities are squarely built but does so on the basis of a prophetic critique coming primarily from Christian communities in the Third World!

11. The reference is to Christopher Jencks and David Riesman, *The Academic Revolution* (Garden City, NY: Doubleday, 1968), which chronicled the ascendancy of an academic "professionalism" (i.e., elitism) that was sweeping everything before it, including the values cherished by church-related schools (p. 327).

12. This collapse coincided with the waning of the "Biblical Theology" movement on which it had been based as well as the loss of momentum in the Protestant ecumenical movement which had largely sponsored the "Christian University Movement" as described above. For a personal reminiscence of this collapse, with special reference to the Presbyterian Church in the United States of America, see Robert Wood Lynn, "'The Survival of Recognizably Protestant Colleges': Reflections on Old-Line Protestantism, 1950-1990," *The Secularization of the Academy*, edited by George M. Marsden and Bradley J. Longfield (New York: Oxford University Press, 1992), 170-194.

13. Claude Welch, *Graduate Education in Religion* (Missoula: University of Montana Press, 1971). Not only does Welch never mention any efforts to bring the influence of the Christian faith to bear on higher education, but he also ignores the possible benefits of graduate education in religion for communities of faith. It is as if the two worlds of church and university were hermetically sealed off from each other. For an extended critique see William E. Hull, "Graduate Education in a Denominational Seminary," *Review and Expositor* 70 (Winter, 1973), 49-61.

14. Citing the establishment of the Christian College Consortium in 1971 and the Christian College Coalition in 1976 see Robert Wood Lynn, "'The Survival of Recognizably Protestant Colleges': Reflections on Old-Line Protestantism, 1950-1990," *The Secularization of the Academy*, edited by George M. Marsden and Bradley J. Longfield (New York: Oxford University Press, 1992), 187.

15. I am here using "fundamentalism" as both a religious and a cultural category, and am doing so in a descriptive rather than a pejorative sense. On its origins and early history see George M. Marsden, *Fundamentalism and American Culture. The Shaping of Twentieth-Century Evangelicalism:* 1870-1925 (New York: Oxford University Press, 1980). On the efforts of fundamentalism in the '20s to oppose prohibition, evolution, and Roman Catholicism (Al Smith as president), and the negative effects of these campaigns, see Kenneth K. Bailey, *Southern White Protestantism in the Twentieth Century* (New York: Harper and Row, 1964), esp. 44-110. The effort to recast fundamentalism into evangelicalism began in 1947 with a book by Carl F.H. Henry, *The Uneasy Conscience of Modern Fundamentalism* (Grand Rapids: Wm. B. Eerdmans, 1947). However, the resurgence of classic fundamentalism began around 1975 with the rise of New Right Religion. On the international dimensions of fundamentalism as a cultural phenomenon see the five-volume work of *The Fundamentalism Project* edited by Martin E. Marty and R. Scott Appleby (Chicago: University of Chicago Press, 1991-95). Education is treated in volume 2, *Fundamentalism and Society: Reclaiming the Sciences, the Family, and Education* (1993), 311-573.

16. A flood of literature traces the connection between right-wing politics and right-wing religion. For a selection see Richard Pienard, "Bibliography on the New Christian Right," *TSF Bulletin* (November/December 1981), s1-s4. Most significant in forging the alliance between fundamentalism and politics was Jerry Falwell. See the book written primarily by Ed Dobson and Ed Hindson which he edited, *The Fundamentalist Option: The Resurgence of Conservative Christianity* (Garden City, NY: Doubleday, 1981). On the larger story, see William Martin, *With God on Our Side: The Rise of the Religious Right in America* (New York: Broadway Books, 1996).

17. On the religious roots of American anti-intellectualism, see Richard Hofstadter, *Anti-intellectualism in American Life* (New York: Knopf, 1970), 53-141.

18. See Roland Mushat Frye, editor, *Is God a Creationist? The Religious Case Against Creation-Science* (New York: Scribner's, 1984); Ronald L. Numbers, *The Creationists* (New York: Alfred A. Knopf, 1992).

19. See Willis B. Glover, *The Biblical Origins of Modern Secular Culture* (Macon: Mercer University Press, 1984).

20. See William E. Hull, *Conservatism and Liberalism: A Christian Critique*, The Derwood W. Deere Lectures (Mill Valley, CA: Golden Gate Baptist Theological Seminary, 1983).
21. See Christopher Lasch, *The Culture of Narcissism* (New York: W.W. Norton, 1978).
22. Mark A. Noll, "The Scandal of the Evangelical Mind," McManis Installation Lecture, Wheaton College (February 9, 1993) 6-7. For a summary see his "The Scandal of the Evangelical Mind," *Christianity Today* (October 25, 1993) 29-32.
23. Mark A. Noll, *The Scandal of the Evangelical Mind* (Grand Rapids: William B. Eerdmans, 1994), 51.
24. Page Smith, *Killing the Spirit: Higher Education in America* (New York: Viking, 1990).
25. H. Richard Niebuhr, *Christ and Culture*, Harper Torchbooks (New York: Harper & Brothers, 1951).
26. Jencks and Riesman, 329-330.
27. Jencks and Riesman, 333.
28. Statistics for 1966-7 are from H.I. Hester, *Southern Baptists in Christian Education* (Murfreesboro, NC: Chowan College, 1968), p. 94. Statistics for 1993 are from *Southern Baptist Handbook 1993* (Nashville: Convention Press, 1993), 101-102, 104-105.
29. Smith, 85.
30. Smith, 86.
31. Smith, 74.
32. Smith, 87-88.

CHAPTER 3
Education as Sabbath

Earl Palmer

I have a text. I am in good company to do that because most universities have a text, found most often in the school's emblem and symbol. It often surprises people to learn that even the great public universities often have biblical texts. For example, the symbol of the University of California has the Bible right in the middle of the university crest! Then, around it are the words, "Let there be light." That is right out of Genesis! The University of California even has a hymn, "O God, Our Help in Ages Past." Or another example is, "Ye shall know the truth and the truth shall set you free," the motto of Columbia University's emblem.

Therefore, it is only appropriate to have a text as we think about Christian higher education. However, one might be a little surprised with this text. It is an Old Testament text about me, about man/woman, my relationship with the earth, my relationship with God, and my relationship with myself. And certainly that is what the university is all about. Without question that is what a church-related, Christian college or university should be about: my relationship with God, my relationship with the earth, my relationship with myself, and my relationship with my neighbor. There are four great relationships in this text.

Because this text has been difficult to interpret in its journey through the Old and New Testaments, it might surprise you. It happens to be the Fourth Commandment. I call this "a Commandment for the Christian University."

> Observe the Sabbath day by keeping it holy, as the LORD your
> God has commanded you. Six days you shall labor and do all

your work, but the seventh day is a Sabbath to the Lord your
God. On it you shall not do any work, neither you, nor your son
or daughter, nor your manservant or maidservant, nor your ox,
your donkey or any of your animals, nor the alien within your
gates, so that your manservant and your maidservant may rest
as you do. Remember that you were slaves in Egypt and that
the LORD your God brought you out of there with a mighty
hand and an outstretched arm. Therefore the Lord your God
has commanded you to observe the Sabbath day" (Deuteronomy
5:12-15).[1]

There are several important words or phrases in this passage. First, it is
important to know that Sabbath comes from "Shabat" which means "to
cease" or literally "seven." Remember that in the Hebrew language words
often serve double duty and can mean several things. It can also mean
"rest" so that there is some play on the word's meaning. Second, it is important to recognize the wide-reaching implications of the command. It touches
the animal kingdom and, as we know from other scripture, extends to include the land. This is a command which impacts not only relationships,
work and worship; it impacts our ecology.

You will remember that this commandment is also found in Exodus 20.
It is slightly different in the Exodus passage because the "remember" reads,
"You shall remember that God created the earth well." So in Exodus, we
are reminded to remember creation while in Deuteronomy we're reminded
to remember redemption. If you put them together, you're to remember
that God made the earth, and He made it well, and you will remember that
God redeemed you.

I think the fourth commandment is a great commandment for a Christian university because of several mandates which emerge from it. However, before I examine these let me say a few things about the edges of the
command that are very important for us to understand. Notice that the
command describes your life in terms of seven days; it describes your life as
"boundaried" within seven days. I've often said to myself, "You could make

sense out of your life, and you can protect your life from burnout if you realize your life in terms of seven days." You've got to have your seven days make sense.

Don't talk to me about "this month I'll do something," or "next year I'm going to do something," because I have to make sense out of seven days. And that's where the command describes you: sensible, down-to-earth, realistic, do-able, and rhythmic. It is a rhythmic command: a command about the rhythm between work and rest within seven days. Boundaried and rhythmic. That's the nature of this command.

It's also a freedom command. It's a continuation of an understanding about the "boundaried freedom" that God gives us in Genesis. We are to find our work; we are to find our rest. The command doesn't say, "Six days of the week you will be available for work if someone can find work for you," or "The seventh day you will rest if your family can force you to rest." Oh, no. "Six days you shall work." Find your work, and you must find your rest. I'm not treated like a victim, but like someone who should be proactive, not reactive. So it's a proactive, freedom command. I should find my work. I should find my rest within seven days.

Faculty, students, staff, do that, and you'll keep your sanity. Do that and you will not burn out. I know! I've been a pastor long enough to listen to people tell lots of burnout stories. Burnout happens when every day looks alike, and there's no sense of boundary except for next Christmas when the whole family's going to have a wonderful time. That does not work! You may remember W.H. Auden's comment about Christmas, "Ah, yes, that time of the year when we all try unsuccessfully to love all our relatives."[2] You can't put that much pressure on Christmas break! You've got to make seven days boundaried, and you will not burn out. Then you can fulfill your mandate.

One of the chief problems in our culture, our colleges and our churches is that everybody's burning out. So many people are dealing with stress, breakdown and loss of purpose or direction. We must learn a sense of perspective, boundary and limits. What a great lesson students would learn if they took from their college education a sense of rhythm, balance, boundary and equilibrium. It would serve them their whole life!

At the heart of this commandment are three mandates for church-related higher education. The first mandate has to do with the first part of the commandment: "Six days thou shalt labor." The first task of a Christian university — of any university — is the work task. The work is to help men and women become prepared for a lifetime of work. The university is where they begin to discern the contribution they can make and where they are equipped to do it.

You have to feel good about your head, and you have to feel good about your hands if you work. And a college or university has an unforgettable, nonnegotiable mandate to help a man or woman find work. In other words, the first task of a first-class liberal arts university is to train people to think clearly, to use their brains, to express and write down what they think, i.e., be able to do something well with their hands, minds and hearts.

I love C.S. Lewis' wonderful little book, *Experiment in Criticism*,[3] which is probably the best book about a liberal arts education ever written. He wrote it just a year before he died. It's not a religious book. It is a book about how to read a book.

In it he draws a distinction between two kinds of people: the serious man who plays football and the serious football player. The serious football player plays football not so much for the calories it will burn and not so much for exercise, but for the love of the sport. "I *want* to play football." That is a serious football player. On the other hand, the serious man or woman plays football in order to get exercise, in order to use up calories, or for some reason other than the joy of the sport itself.

Lewis takes this little parable and relates it to being a literate person. A serious reader is a person who has been brought into and under a book, reads a book, lets the story flow over him/her, engages the story and the book, and becomes genuinely literate, reading books because he/she loves them and the ideas within them. That is what a liberal arts education does. It gives you a love of books, letters and ideas, so that you will know how to think clearly, write clearly and speak clearly. As a result, others will understand what you believe, think and how you live.

Therefore the university's task is to help you put it all together and integrate it with your hands and feet so that you can do something with it. So for six days of each week you are doing something that you can do, that you want to do, and that makes a contribution to our world.

Several years ago Stephen Hawking spoke on astrophysics at the University of California. Four lecture halls were filled with listeners. This professor, the Sir Isaac Newton Professor of Theoretical Physics at Cambridge University, will probably someday win the Nobel Prize for Physics by creating a unified theory which pulls all of physics together. [4]

The story of Stephen Hawking's life is a very interesting one. He contracted ALS, a muscle disease, in the middle of his adult life, and it progressively weakened him to the point that he now cannot speak. He has to type out his words, and a synthesizer voice speaks for him. When he was a younger man, he was not physically impaired in any way. He attended Oxford University and quickly became bored. Hawking tells the story of how in that boredom he became addicted to alcohol, drinking heavily every day and losing all interest in school. He began to fail in his grades and in his schoolwork. In fact, when he took exams, he would mock professors by creating questions they couldn't answer to go alongside the questions they were creating for him. His mind was absolutely brilliant, but he was bored. [5]

Hawking, whose life was beginning to fall apart and literally spin out of control because of alcohol and boredom at Oxford, was turned around by one professor. As the story is told, this professor called him into his office, realizing that Hawking had no direction and was not being challenged.

"Hawking, I have a project I want you to do," the professor started. "I want you to solve for me black holes."

"Black holes?" Hawking replied.

"You could be the one, now go to it," the professor concluded.

Stephen Hawking has commited the rest of his life to trying to solve black holes. [6]

Hawking's book *A Brief History of Time* is stunning. I still do not have the slightest idea what the chapter on black holes means, but I have read it three times! It is known as the book that has made physics accessible, a physics user-friendly book. Hawking tries to explain his unified theory and black holes. It is his passion and consuming desire.

But you know something, that young mind was about ready to be a wasted mind until a first-rate professor had a first-rate idea. He gave that young mind a challenge of a work to do that was just so big that from that moment on it so captivated Hawking that he was never bored another day.

Soon after, he contracted ALS, but still it did not stop his dedication. Colleges, universities and professors should be about the business of helping students to find a problem and identify a "work" that can capture their life's energy.

The second mandate, antiphonal to labor, is to help one find rest. If there's a straining at the boundaries, a need to know, a need to learn and a need to do, then the flipside of the fourth commandment is one of peace and rest. It was Saint Augustine who fully understood this when he ended his great confession by saying, "O God, Thou Who art ever at work and ever at rest, may I be ever at work and ever at rest." There is an antiphonal balance in the fourth commandment. This must never be trivialized by little tricky hoops about what constitutes work and what constitutes rest. That is where previous generations of Christians, like the Pharisees, have often gone wrong. In every week we need a rhythm of work and rest.

A great university needs rhythm. If one side of the rhythm is the intensity of giving oneself to work ... the other side is learning how to rest. It's the friendship building. It's the relaxed, *sheer fun* side of the rhythmic balance present in every great school.

Every school should not only be a hard, salty, tough workplace; it should also be fun. Students are going to like this part, and I hope faculty and staff do, too. Because today one of the great tasks of a great university is to help young men and women find friends, friends that will last the rest of their lives. People who they can settle down with in a friendship where they don't have to play any games. Unlike T.S. Eliot's line, "to put on a face to meet the face that you meet."[7] You can be at peace with these friends, and there can be a kind of peace and gentleness in your soul. And here's a place where you find and reveal the real you. I know many faculty also in need of this. In fact so do administrators, staff, trustees. We all need it.

There's an intense loneliness in our culture. In fact, there are many kinds of loneliness. There is a loneliness because of discontentedness, a lack of a sense of being part of something bigger than one's self. That is part of what institutions can provide. Even the technology of communication can make us lonely! Do you realize one can live a whole week, and because of voice mail never have one conversation with a living human being at the other end of the phone? Do you get the message?

My wife got a message on voice mail from a friend the other day. Her friend said, "Now Shirley, you and Earl are going to come over to dinner and I'm going to make the steaks. You bring the salads. No, no, no, no, don't, don't do that. No, you bring the desserts, I'll take care of the salads. Well, no, that is not right. You and Earl are going out afterward to another meeting where they're going to have dessert, so, hey, cancel that. Don't bring dessert. Just bring salad. We won't have the dessert at all. Is that OK? That should be fine." It was like a conversation! She just made up a conversation with the voice mail! Technology can lead us to a certain kind of loneliness.

Peaceableness with friends is a key ingredient to discovering what it means to be at rest. That is why I favor students settling into a college, spending four years there if at all possible, and not living at home. (I realize that because these are ideals, sometimes finances, family or other circumstances may prohibit.) Most of us do not make lifelong friends in weeks; friendship takes time and energy.

Great colleges and universities care about the kind of settings where friends can be discovered, nurtured and built. This requires reasonable workloads. Faculty are wrong to think that academics is all that education is about. Colleges need to have the kind of housing that encourages real friendship building, and loads of on-campus jobs that enable students to work, study and play together. A great university will create the kind of atmosphere where you can fraternize, where you can sit around and exchange ideas, test out personal goals, reflect on what is being learned. These can be important ingredients in an institution hoping to create an environment where people's lives are impacted and changed.

The third mandate of a great university is to help students remember. The command in the fourth commandment, the big command, is "you shall remember!" Remember, God made the earth well and God redeemed us. Creation and redemption.

It is no small challenge to suggest that institutions be Christian without apology. Don't be a college with just a dose of religiosity thrown in. Too many church-related schools act as if religion is just one more phenomena to be studied. Don't do that. Don't just be a cafeteria of ideas. It is far better to have professors who feel keenly and intensely about ideas, even ideas which produce tension, than to act as if all ideas have equal merit. One can do so much of one's ideological, theological and spiritual formation in an atmosphere where one really has to think through ideas while being related to honestly and allowed to struggle with the great ideas of human history.

But, do you have convictions? Is that text at the heart of the institution's emblem? Christian colleges should have convictions and honestly affirm them. Affirm them with respect for young men, women and colleagues inside and outside the university. We're in a pluralistic society. In a pluralistic society, the only kind of tolerance for other people that really matters is a tolerance that comes from a person who has convictions.

When you have convictions and a mission you believe in, and you seek to adhere faithfully to that mission, then you can be tolerant and respectful of people with whom you don't agree. That is a tolerance that means something. Not tolerance that says, "Hey, you just do your thing; I'm doing mine ... nothing really matters that much after all, does it?" That kind of vapid relativism is not a tolerance of any substance. We need people who have strong convictions. We need institutions where there is a commitment to share at the center ... to work from a shared purpose. Christian colleges must not assume that the students from churches have any sense of our great Christian heritage. We must seek to share that heritage, to acquaint them with the great history of our faith and to remember God's faithfulness throughout the generations.

About four years ago, our family had a tremendous lifelong dream fulfilled. We took a trip across Russia on the Trans-Siberian Railroad. When we got to Leningrad the big thing that I wanted my family to see was the Hermitage Museum — the greatest museum in the whole world — a thousand-room palace that Katherine the Great had built. There are more Rembrandts in the Hermitage than any other museum in the world. Everything is there ... Renoir, Monet, El Greco ... many of the world's greatest works of art.

So we went to this museum. We had a little guide who was very militant. Our family was her only group ... just our five. Still, she held up a card to show where we were going! She whipped us into shape and gave us lectures on all of the art. It was wonderful! She knew everything! She showed us these different paintings and commented on this and that. It was an education because she had been a guide for eight years and knew every single painting. She saved the Rembrandt Room for last, and I was glad because Rembrandt is my hero.

We looked at the paintings as she explained them. She was proudest of the Rembrandt collection, especially the great Rembrandt painting titled, "Return of the Prodigal," which was found in his room at his death. She showed the hands of the father, pointing out that art critics around the world would probably call this the greatest portrayal of hands in all of art ... the father's hands on the shoulders of the boy. The hands were liberating hands, not gripping or clutching hands. Absolutely marvelous! Then we saw this strange unfinished figure standing to the side, gripping a staff. Though we are not sure, it was most likely the elder brother.

Then she said, "Notice the blind father as he blesses his son."

I said, "*What?*"

She said, "Well, notice the blind father as he blesses his son, because you see the painting is the father down here blessing the boy."

So I said to her, "No, that's not right." Now this took a lot of courage! It took a lot of courage in my blood because, to remind you, she "knew" these paintings. But I said, "No, no, that's not right."

Then I dared to recite to her the parable of the prodigal son, the basis of this painting. Knowing that Rembrandt was a great biblical expositor in his paintings, I said, "This is the parable of the prodigal son." I told her the parable ... how the boy went away and then the boy came back. While the lad was a long way away, the father saw him, and had compassion on him (I said this very slowly to her) and he ran to the boy and embraced him. In fact, the good eyesight of the father is very critical to this parable, because if the elder brother had seen the boy first, he'd have never made it home! That's the whole point. The father's eyesight is so good, he sees the boy a long way off. We later discover the elder brother doesn't think anything of this younger brother.

The father goes out into the dark to find the elder son hiding in the darkness sulking with self-righteousness — self-righteousness puts you in darkness, too. When he finds him he says, "Son, all that I have is yours, and you will always be with me. But this is right that we have this party, because your brother was dead and now he is alive." What an amazing parable!

I told it to her, and then she said, "Oh." She did not argue with me. She said, "Oh," and that was all.

My children, two college students and one high school student, and I talked about this guide. Her English was flawless, and she was brilliant, and her specialty was American student groups. I imagined that if she took one tour a day for these eight years and American student groups were her main group, and she always saved the Rembrandt Room for last because she held the most pride in the Rembrandts ... then probably for eight years

... every day to a group of students ... she said, "Now look at the blind father as he blesses his son." For at least eight years she got it wrong to hundreds of people.

She didn't know the parable of the prodigal son. She probably got it mixed up with another account in the Old Testament of a father who was tricked by his son into blessing him. Can you see what a tragedy it is that for eight years these students have been coming, and she has been saying, "Look at the blind father as he blesses his son." Evidently no one has countered her. And then we figured out why. Do you know why? *Because no one in those groups of students apparently knew the difference! They didn't know!* Allen Bloom says so in his *Closing of the American Mind.* "American students don't enjoy the art galleries of Europe because you have to know *the Bible* to know the art galleries of Europe!"[8]

They didn't know. And because they didn't know, they missed the most incredible truth about the gospel of Jesus Christ, that *God* has good eyesight. He isn't tricked into blessing us. He knows all about us. He knows about a boy who's hurting and wandering out there, wondering if he's worth anything. And then he's found and is blessed. He knows about a sulking, self-righteous boy, and He finds him. That's the Father that Jesus is describing.

What a tragedy for students and others who mix up the parable of the prodigal son with the Old Testament story of the blind father Isaac and his sons Jacob and Esau. What else did they miss in their education because they didn't know the basic stories of faith?

We have a task at a Christian university to teach people the truth about God's redemption and God's creation ... the goodness of creation. It is a tremendous challenge to teach about the earth and to teach it accurately. There are no advantages to ignorance. At a Christian university one should hear about God's love so that we can remember it and know it. It certainly will not be a part of the educational experience at "State University" even if they do still have the Bible in their emblem or motto!

I recently read a review of a book by a Yale ethicist, who took 25 students into a room. (They were all college freshmen at this Ivy League university.) He asked them one question: "Can you construct for me the Ten Commandments?" These 25 students (you can imagine what their SAT scores are) could not reconstruct the Ten Commandments. They simply didn't know them.

He was pointing this out as an example of why there is a kind of ethical vacuum in our culture. It is because no one knows these things anymore. We don't remember them. I believe one of the great mandates of a church-related university is to help us remember the truth which is at the foundation of every unique institution.

Perhaps the best way to communicate the point I am making is in a poem I wrote for our youngest daughter when she went away to college. It is called "Remembering." I offer it as a kind of statement on what higher learning should be.

> Remembering my friends, who I loved in the simpler times
> of youth, will help me be a friend;
>
> Remembering the songs and the shows that they go with
> (my daughter loved musicals) makes new songs easier to learn;
>
> Remembering my home as the place always for me makes
> me more at home when I'm away;
>
> Remembering my name and the dreams I made my own
> gives me strength when people wonder who I am;
>
> Remembering the love that found me before I could
> remember keeps life alive while I am remembering.

A considerable challenge and a substantial mandate is before those colleges and universities that aspire to true greatness. Those institutions that help us learn to work, rest and remember will be recognized as places that have an eternal impact on people's lives. Let those who have ears, hear.

ENDNOTES

1. Holy Bible, *New International Version*, Deuteronomy 5:12-15 (Grand Rapids: Zondervan, 1984).
2. Edward Mendelson, ed., *Collected Poems of W.H. Auden* (New York: Vintage International, Vintage Books, 1991).
3. C.S. Lewis, *Experiment in Criticism* (Cambridge [England]: University Press, 1961).
4. Vicki Braden, prod. "Stephen Hawking: The Universe Within" (Burlington, NC: Cardin Biological Supply Co. videorecording, 1989).
5. Ibid.
6. S.W. Hawking, *A Brief History of Time* (Toronto/New York: Bantam, 1988).
7. J.L. Dawson, ed., *The Complete Poems and Plays of T.S. Eliot* (Ithaca, NY: Cornell University Press, 1995).
8. Alan Bloom, *The Closing of the American Mind* (New York: Simon & Schuster, 1987).

CHAPTER 4
Integration and Conversation

Harold Heie

It appears to me that our culture is increasingly characterized by fragmentation and polarization. What especially alarms me as a Christian educator is that I see such fragmentation and polarization rapidly increasing in Christian subcultures. In light of this, my vision for Christian higher education has two primary foci: integration (as an antidote to fragmentation) and conversation (as a remedy for polarization).

The integration focus is something we have talked about for a long time in Christian higher education, but our rhetoric has far outdistanced our performance. We need to be called back to this old focus. The conversation focus is an exciting new possibility for Christian higher education, if we have the will and courage to pursue it. I start with three dimensions for the integrative ideal.

Integration: Two Worlds of Knowledge

The first dimension is the integration of two worlds of knowledge. My strong convictions about this ideal can only be captured if I share some background. I grew up intellectually in two worlds of knowledge that never intersected: two airtight compartments, an impenetrable wall between them.

I became a Christian as a teen-ager in a revival meeting in the basement of a Norwegian Lutheran church in Brooklyn, NY (back in the days when the Dodgers were the Brooklyn Dodgers). I then fell under the influence of a godly Sunday school teacher who inspired me to immerse myself in the Scriptures. I devoured the pages of my Bible as I sought to better understand myself and my confusing world of adolescence. I thereby came to love my first world of knowledge, my world of biblical understanding. As I grew intellectually, it expanded into my world of biblical and theological understanding.

During these same years of formation, a second world of knowledge was developing, the world of knowledge from the academic disciplines. As I studied first in the natural sciences, and then later more informally in the humanities and social sciences, I also grew to love knowledge in the academic disciplines.

But my two worlds of knowledge never met. The secular universities I attended cared little about my world of biblical theological understanding. And my church was fearful of my world of academic disciplinary knowledge, concerned that it might contaminate my biblical and theological understanding. So my knowledge was hopelessly fragmented, like that of most Christians I knew then, and know now — even highly educated Christians, including some Christians teaching at Christian institutions of higher education.

I knew that such fragmentation of knowledge was inadequate, though I didn't have a clue at that time how to overcome it. It was then like a breath of fresh air to discover that Christian liberal arts colleges were committed, at least in words, to that distinctive vision of integrating my two worlds of knowledge. That's when I knew that I would devote my professional life to Christian liberal arts education.

Now, more than 30 years later, that ideal of integrating my two worlds of knowledge still drives me. I have, however, painfully discovered that much of that integrative talk is just meant for the first few pages of the college catalog. For example, for something that is supposedly so important, it is amazing how little time and other resources Christian colleges give to faculty members to pursue this arduous integrative task. Talk is cheap! If you want to discover a college's priorities, don't read the first few pages of the college catalog, read the annual budget.

Nevertheless, the ideal still burns within me. The most fundamental distinctive of Christian liberal arts education is the integration of knowledge: the search for interrelationships between biblical and theological understanding and knowledge in the academic disciplines, the quest for a coherent system of thought that establishes connections between these two worlds such that each illuminates, complements and enriches the other.

I claim that such integrated knowledge is a realizable ideal for any academic discipline, even my teaching discipline of mathematics, when one digs beneath the surface to the deep level of the subject matter, the level of fundamental philosophical assumptions.

I believe that every discipline is informed by ontological assumptions, often implicit and unexamined, assumptions about the entities that the discipline works with, whether they be electrons, social groups, numbers, written texts or living organisms. But ontological assumptions are also part of my biblical and theological understanding. Therein resides more potential for illuminating connections.

And I also believe that every discipline is informed by axiological assumptions about what is of value. Every discipline is informed by value commitments. But value commitments are also part of my biblical and theological understanding. Therein resides still more potential for illuminating connections.

So there! I've said it again, for what seems like the millionth time. And I'm going to keep saying it until more people listen, including more college presidents and members of college governing boards. The integration of knowledge is the most distinctive task of Christian liberal arts education — always was, is now, always will be.

The Central Importance of Christian Scholarship

As a corollary to the claim I just made, let me say a few words about the importance of Christian scholarship. If a Christian college or university really believes in the ideal of integrating my two worlds of knowledge, then the next logical step is for that institution to provide the time and resources that faculty need to do first-order scholarship informed by Christian presuppositions and perspectives. But very few Christian institutions of higher education are willing to do that.

I think that such Christian institutions need to create a viable middle ground between two unacceptable extremes. At one extreme are those research universities where you publish or perish, where devoting considerable time and energy to good teaching may hinder your professional advancement. For me that is an unacceptable extreme.

But equally unacceptable to me is the other extreme — the typical Christian college model — where faculty have such heavy teaching, advising and institutional service responsibilities that there is no time left for first-order scholarship. I've seen many potential Christian scholars dry up because they came to teach at Christian institutions of higher education. That is also unacceptable to me.

We need to create an environment for faculty where they can be both effective teachers and effective scholars.

My call for Christian colleges to foster high-quality scholarship on the part of their faculty often elicits the question "What's in it for the student?" I have two answers, the first of which makes some sense to many questioners, but the second of which often elicits blank stares of disbelief.

First, the potential for quality education is greatly increased when a student is mentored by a teacher and scholar, a faculty member who exemplifies that the quest for further knowledge is a never-ending task for both student and teacher.

So far, so good! It's my second answer that is a shocker to many, including some ultimately responsible for governing Christian colleges. It is integral to one's calling as a Christian educator that one share with the larger academic community the results of first-order scholarship informed by Christian perspectives. The larger academic community desperately needs to be exposed to this type of scholarship. And Christian scholars teaching at Christian colleges need to produce and disseminate such scholarship. That task is the Christian scholar's witness as "salt" and "light" in the larger academy.

As George Marsden has put it, we need to penetrate that highest level of the critical thought of culture and offer thoroughly Christian wisdom for public application. And that takes significant resource allocation without compensating tuition dollars. That is one reason why we seldom commit ourselves to this ideal for Christian scholarship. A more fundamental reason is that we are often so attuned to seeking immediate results from our evangelical activism that we grossly undervalue the potential long-term benefits of Christian thinking that could help shape the future direction of our culture. This needs to change! Scholarship informed by Christian perspectives is kingdom work, just like evangelism is. Such Christian scholarship needs generous support from administrators, trustees and donors.

An Integrated Spirituality

A second dimension of my integrative ideal is a broad view of spirituality that is truly integrated. On many Christian college campuses, there has been a healthy increase in interest, on the part of a number of students and faculty, in matters pertaining to spiritual formation. There is a healthy increase of interest in serious cocurricular study of the Bible, in personal and corporate prayer, in gathering together to sing songs of praise to God.

I endorse this increased interest in what I will call Spirituality A, the many time-honored ways in which we as Christians are called to celebrate and give expression to our Christian faith. But there is also a dark side to this increased interest in Spirituality A, a pernicious tendency toward fragmentation, a tendency to bifurcate Spirituality A from other legitimate expressions of spirituality (that I will soon call Spirituality B and Spirituality C).

I'll illustrate this danger with a personal example. At one Christian college where I served as chief academic officer, our first chapel each fall was an honors convocation, in which we celebrated academic gifts and I gave a brief meditation on some theme that sought to relate Christian commitment to the importance of intellectual inquiry. A few days before one of these honors convocations, I got wind of the fact that a particular student planned to disrupt the convocation by standing up in the middle of my meditation and proclaiming to the audience that a meditation on intellectual matters has no place in a chapel, for, after all, chapel is where we come together to worship God. What a terrible, demonic bifurcation. (By the way, I immediately called that student into my office. I don't think I changed his mind, but he didn't disrupt my meditation.)

For me, the life of the mind is not peripheral to my spirituality; it is integral to my spirituality. The quest for understanding the nature of God's creation, through integration of my two worlds of knowledge, is a spiritual quest (my Spirituality B). For me, it is an expression of worship. I worship God as much in my study as I do in my church.

But there is a second insidious tendency toward spiritual bifurcation, a tendency to divorce spirituality from a commitment to serving other people, a tendency toward privatization of religion, where the goal is to "feel good about yourself." Hear the timeless warning of the prophet Amos (5:21-24):

> "I hate, I despise your religious feasts; I cannot stand your assemblies. Even though you bring me burnt offerings and grain offerings, I will not accept them. Though you bring choice fellowship offerings, I will have no regard for them. Away with the noise of your songs! I will not listen to the music of your harps. But let justice roll on like a river, righteousness like a never-failing stream!"

Doing justice, compassionately attending to the needs of other people, especially the disenfranchised and the powerless, is an integral aspect of my understanding of spirituality (my Spirituality C).

I am dismayed at the extent to which self-help pop psychology has invaded Christian thinking, easily leading to a spiritual narcissism. "I'm OK, you're OK" is not the message of the gospel. The message of the gospel is "I'm not OK, but that's OK"; that's God's grace. And if you have experienced that overwhelming grace, you will be empowered to love other people, even when, or especially when, they're not OK.

The desire to "feel good about yourself" will remain elusive if you seek it as an end in itself. I'm all for you "feeling good about yourself." But that is a by-product of pouring yourself out in service to other people.

In summary, I say "yes" to an increased emphasis on spirituality. But it must be an integrated spirituality: a spirituality that expresses itself in Bible study, prayer and the singing of spiritual songs; but also a spirituality that expresses itself in serving other people as an agent of reconciliation in a broken world.

Personal Integration

A third dimension of integration is personal integration. A person must be viewed holistically, as one who thinks, feels, worships something, plays, relates to others and has a body that needs caring for.

The classical emphasis of liberal arts education on the liberating effect of cognitive understanding is good, as far as it goes, but such a view of liberation is too narrow. Persons are not disembodied intellects. What about the intellectual giant who no longer marvels at the sight of a sunset, who no longer weeps when a friend is hurting, who no longer has any deeply felt experience of the grace and presence of God? He too must be liberated.

Of course the primary business of college is learning. A college cannot be all things to all persons (e.g., a church or a health spa). But a college can and ought to help students learn about all aspects of their whole beings. A third fundamental integrative distinctive of Christian liberal arts education is personal integration, helping each student learn about and experience developments of his/her whole being.

That is my integrative vision: Integration of Two Worlds of Knowledge, An Integrated Spirituality, Personal Integration. We still talk a lot about it. But we need to do much more of it. As we approach the end of this century, we need to recommit ourselves to this old ideal.

But as we continue working on this old ideal, I believe we are also at a challenging time in our cultural history where an exciting new possibility can emerge for Christian higher education, if we have the will and courage to pursue it.

Conversation: Modeling a Community of Inquiry

Dr. C. Everett Koop, former Surgeon General, and Dr. Timothy Johnson, ABC News Medical Editor, co-authored a book, the title of which most eloquently summarizes the proposal I am about to make: *Let's Talk: An Honest Conversation on Critical Issues.*[1] But, as was reported in *Christianity Today,*[2] some Christians in New England didn't want Johnson to talk. When he was invited to speak to the New England Association of Evangelicals, a church group threatened to picket the meeting because they didn't agree with some of the positions Johnson took regarding abortion and euthanasia. So to avoid confrontation and possible bad press for the association, Johnson graciously withdrew from this speaking engagement.

What a tragedy! I especially feel that tragedy because I know Dr. Johnson. He was my associate pastor for five years in a church in West Peabody, MA. No kinder, more thoughtful Christian walks the face of God's earth. But because other Christians disagreed with him, they silenced him. They rejected the kind invitation extended by Drs. Koop and Johnson in the book's preface: "We hope that if you disagree, you will learn from each other's viewpoints, and respect those who differ with you. Let's talk."

There is a cancer that is growing rapidly in the Christian community, the cancer of polarization that ends conversation. The tragedy is not that Christians disagree with each other on some critical issues. In fact, such disagreement can be the bedrock of good education. The tragedy is that we find it increasingly difficult to talk to each other about our disagreements, so that we can learn from each other. Dialogue has too often been replaced by monologue. Conversation has often been replaced by contestation. And this tragedy within the Christian community is just as prominent, if not more so, in our larger American culture.

The great new challenge facing Christian higher education at the end of this century is to create structures that will overcome this insidious drive toward polarization and contestation. In brief, I believe colleges that wish to embrace an evangelical expression of the Christian faith need to create what I call a "middle of the road evangelicalism," somewhere in between fundamentalism and liberalism, that will keep alive the conversation that is necessary for quality Christian education and will model a "community of inquiry" for the Christian community and the larger culture.

Nancy Ammerman, from Emory University, once made the bold suggestion that a potential future contribution of evangelicals to the church and to society is that we create and model "new habits of talking to each other" such that we honestly acknowledge our differences and learn from each other.

But where does one start? I start by situating myself somewhere in between the polar opposites portrayed in descriptions of the much heralded "culture wars." Allow me to illustrate by referring to James Davison Hunter's work *Culture Wars*. Hunter labels the polar opposites as "orthodoxy" and "progressivism," describing these extremes as follows:

> *Orthodoxy* ... is the commitment on the part of adherents to an external, definable, and transcendent authority. Such objective and transcendent authority defines, at least in the abstract, a consistent, unchangeable measure of value, purpose, goodness, and identity, both personal and collective.

By contrast,

> what all *progressivist* world views share in common is the tendency to resymbolize historic faiths according to the prevailing assumptions of contemporary life.[3]

I fit neither extreme, as described above. Although my Christian belief system contains components that I consider unchangeable (e.g., Jesus Christ came into the world to save sinners), I consider many aspects of my present belief system changeable. So if orthodoxy means commitment to a static system of beliefs where my beliefs are unchangeable, then I reject the label of orthodox.

But the progressivist extreme is equally unacceptable to me. Though certain aspects of my Christian belief system are open to continuous refinement and change as I try to make sense of contemporary life and live well here and now, I consider certain aspects of my belief system to transcend particular times and cultures. So if progressivism means total capitulation to the prevailing assumptions of contemporary life, where every belief is subject to change, then I also reject the label of progressivist.

Therefore, I cannot place myself at either extreme, each of which is too simple. Rather, I choose that much more difficult middle ground where I must continuously struggle with the differentiation between beliefs that are unchanging and timeless, and other beliefs that must be open to criticism and refinement at this time and place in history.

But, of course, trying to navigate that middle road begs for me to say something about what a Christian college or university ought to consider unchangeable. I will now enter the lion's den and hint at such a formulation. Since there is much discussion at colleges like ours as to what it means to be an evangelical college, I will start by assuming that the college or university in question wishes to be evangelical. What does that mean? I propose one possible minimalist definition that simply goes back to the root of the word "evangelical": the "evangel," the "good news," the "gospel," "the old, old story of Jesus and His love." If I could create my own evangelical college or university from scratch (which, of course, I probably can't) I would expect faculty to adhere to the following brief evangelical statement:

> Jesus Christ came into the world to save sinners and to redeem
> all of the created order. That "good news" needs to be person-
> ally appropriated and shared with others. Beyond this minimalist
> understanding of being evangelical, I would expect all faculty
> to affirm, together with all Christians, whether evangelical or
> not, a generalized statement of the Christian story that captures
> the major themes of Creation, Fall, Redemption and Consum-
> mation.[4]

This should be a statement that is general enough to allow much room for diversity of interpretation by those immersed in differing theological traditions.

That is the only common theological ground I would expect of all faculty. Everything else should be open for conversation, so that we can learn from each other in a community of inquiry, creating space for a middle-of-the-road dynamic evangelicalism that holds fast to the best in that tradition but is also open to constructive change. Such an evangelical institution of Christian higher education would become what Patricia Beattie Jung has called a "reform school," described as follows:

> On the one hand reform schools are profoundly traditional institutions willing to bear a solitary witness in the world, if necessary, to the truth of their traditions. On the other hand such reform schools are structurally open to the faithful reformation or reconstruction of those same traditions.[5]

Up to this point, my proposal simply creates adequate space for conversation. How does one then facilitate such conversation? Allow me one concrete suggestion. A focal point for my evangelical Christian college or university would be an ongoing public forum devoted to honest conversation about critical contemporary issues. The forum could be titled "Let's Talk." On any given issue, care would be taken to ensure presentation of a diversity of Christian viewpoints, and non-Christian scholars would be invited to join the conversation. By so doing we would be modeling a community of inquiry, a model that is desperately needed in our Christian community as well as in the larger culture.

I close with some reflections on an absolutely indispensable prerequisite if the conversation I call for is to have any hope of taking place.[6] You and I as Christian scholars must be characterized by certain enduring attitudes, variously referred to as Christian virtues or fruits of the spirit.

For example, I can enter into honest conversation with another only if I love that person, which includes trying to put myself in the other person's shoes, trying to see things from her point of view.

I can enter into honest conversation with another only if I am kind and gentle, not trying to "show off" or intellectually "crucify" the person who disagrees with me, but trying to put the best construction on everything she says, and seeking to express my disagreements with kindness.

I can enter into honest conversation with another only if I am patient, recognizing that refining deeply held long-term beliefs is generally a slow process.

Why is there so little honest conversation in our Christian communities and in our larger culture? To a significant extent, it is because there is so little evidence of humility, kindness, gentleness, love and patience.

Therefore, the starting point for conversation is again the "evangel," the "good news," for it is when we are overwhelmed by the good news that Jesus died for our sins that we can be empowered to be humble, kind, gentle, loving and patient.

In conclusion, I propose that integration and conversation are distinctives of Christian higher education worth devoting our lives to as we approach a new century. May God empower us to give expression to these distinctives.

ENDNOTES

1. C. Everett Koop and Timothy Johnson, *Let's Talk: An Honest Conversation on Critical Issues* (Grand Rapids, Zondervan, 1992).
2. *Christianity Today*, March 1993.
3. James Davidson Hunter, *Culture Wars* (New York: Basic Books, 1991), 44-45.
4. Similar to a statement I proposed in H. Heie, "Wanted: Christian Colleges for a Dynamic Evangelicalism," *Christian Scholars Review* (March 1992), 265, 266.
5. S. Hauerwas and J.H. Westerhoff, eds., "A Call for Reform Schools," *Schooling Christians* (Grand Rapids: Eerdmans, 1992), 115.
6. For an elaboration of my reflection, see M.R. Schwehn, *Exiles from Eden* (New York: Oxford University Press, 1993).

CHAPTER 5
Redemptive Learning

Philip W. Eaton

I want to examine how Christians learn and why we need a renewal of learning in the church. It is important that we ask: Does the Christian life require a different kind of learning? Does the Christian life require broad learning at all? Do Christians think differently about the natural world, the great texts of literature and history, the complex issues that plague our political and social environment? Can Christian thinking assist our troubled world that so desperately struggles to find answers?

My answer to these questions is an emphatic and resounding "yes." We must reclaim for learning a vital and vigorous place in the life of the church. Learning should be considered a spiritual discipline, as it has been throughout much of Christian history. Learning should be considered a key component of spiritual formation. At this point in the history of the church, I am convinced we must seek fresh ways to lift up genuine learning in our midst. We must explore in earnest how we think Christianly. We must boldly assert the profound relevance of Christian learning as we shine the light of the gospel into a dark and troubled world. Finally, as we reflect on the crucial place of learning for the future of the church, I think we can make a convincing case that the church's institutions of higher learning hold the greatest promise to teach us how to ground faith, once again, on sound learning.

I want to begin this discussion with a little parable. A good children's sermon, like any good sermon, must have a concrete story from which to explore some kind of theological or spiritual application. Such was the case one Sunday morning as a pastor gathered all the children from the congregation for the children's sermon. He began by talking about a bushy-tailed creature he saw out his kitchen window. This little creature could scamper up a tree with great speed. "I even saw him jump, almost fly, from one tree to another," he said with great excitement. Hoping to make a point about frugality, or planning ahead, the pastor talked about how this little creature prepared for winter by storing food in the tree. "What do you think this little creature is called?" he asked, seeking to engage his curious audience of young learners.

One little guy shot up his hand, and with a clear understanding of the rhetorical strategies of the children's sermon he said, "Well, I'm sure it must be Jesus Christ, but it sounds like a squirrel to me."

I think this little guy's response has much to say about learning in the church and the dilemma Christian educators and scholars face as we seek to think Christianly. We gather around two vitally important commitments. We are most certainly, and passionately, committed to Jesus Christ and His kingdom. And we are just as certainly, even passionately, committed to higher education, which means, in so many different ways, we seek to understand the world and human life through our various disciplines. Now, as Christian thinker, as Christian teachers and scholars, as Christian students, we are faced with a separation, a bifurcation: On the one hand there is Jesus Christ; on the other there is this fascinating, delightful wonder of the squirrel. How we address this bifurcation is absolutely crucial to the future of Christian higher education and the way in which we value and use learning in the church. This is the significant focus for our work on spiritual formation in our Christian colleges and universities. I will venture out quite boldly to say, what we do with the bifurcation that lies at the heart of our experience as Christian learners will define our success as Christian institutions of higher learning in the days to come.

We talk often about integration, our way of responding to this troubling bifurcation. There are huge numbers of conferences on the integration of faith and learning. Some institutions even include in criteria for promotion and tenure evidence of the ability to integrate a vital Christian life with strong scholarship. But I am afraid just as often we seek the safety of separation. Keep the classroom and the chapel at different ends of the campus, please. As scholars, we seek credibility in the guild of our disciplines. That often seems to require that we check our Christian commitments at the door of the study. After all, if I try integrating faith into my scholarship, I will have difficulty becoming published, at least in the important journals of my discipline. Promotion and tenure, even at our Christian colleges and universities, require that I publish, and that leaves me no choice but to maintain separation of faith and learning in my scholarship.

Besides, it is risky business to bring my faith into vital and vigorous conversation with my discipline. Serious thinking as a Christian may change the way I do my work as a sociologist, a literary critic or a biologist. I have invested a good portion of my life to become a scholar, and I seek respectability. My faith poses some threat. Better to keep a little quiet, at least intellectually, when it comes to matters of faith. On the other hand, my discipline just may threaten my faith. After all, the world's wisdom, of which I am truly an expert in my field, denies almost all of the fundamental assumptions dear to my faith.

It is indeed dangerous to seek serious conversation across the gap of this bifurcation. We are in a dangerous business as Christian educators. Most often we are left pondering a huge gap between Jesus Christ on the one hand and the squirrel on the other. I suspect our little boy on Sunday morning made his statement with some measure of skepticism, a little weary and wary about artificially bringing these two dimensions together. And we must share the little boy's skepticism. Indeed, because we should not artificially bring the two together, we are left with the quandary of bifurcation. Let me repeat: This bifurcation of Jesus and the squirrel, the safe and convenient separation of faith and learning, is the most serious threat to the future of Christian higher education. I would venture to say as well it is a serious threat to the future of the church. We must seek to close the gap. We must find our way to vital faith and vigorous intellectual reflection. We cannot afford bifurcation. This is our high calling. How we teach and model ourselves as learners for our students, for the world and for the church, how we send our graduates into the world and the church as thinking Christians, is absolutely central to the mission of our colleges and universities and will help give shape to the church's future.

How can we answer this question: What good is learning to the Christian? Why go to a Christian college? Why not just prepare for a practical vocation and have done with it? Why not a fine secular institution where the bifurcation of faith and learning is not even an issue, where suspicion rests solely on the faith side of the equation?

The Apostle Paul has done some very significant thinking on these questions; I might even venture to call it "Paul's plan for higher learning." Paul, most certainly an intellectual himself, trained in all the best Jewish "universities" of his time, had reflected on just our dilemma. He knew the quandary of bifurcation, and he provides us with quite a remarkable solution. In Paul's first great letter to the Corinthians, especially the first two chapters, we find a powerful discourse on Christian learning. I think we find here clear direction for the work of Christian educators.

Paul's foundational position is that Jesus Christ transforms our way of viewing the world. The "word of the cross" is his language here, and this radical "word" fundamentally changes the way we learn. As Christians, we have first of all a different epistemology, a different way of knowing, a distinctive vision, a radically unique perspective. We can't help but learn differently. The "word of the cross" changes everything. We stand in a certain place (that is the root meaning of epistemology) because of the cross and view the world from that distinctive, profoundly different place.

We can say at the outset that Paul's reflections with the Corinthians, actually his debate with his church, is vitally relevant to our work as Christian educators. The Corinthian world shares many characteristics with our postmodern world. The Corinthian Christians were surrounded by a quintessentially secular, prosperous, materialistic and radically pluralistic society. It is clear they were drawn to the intellectual trends of the day: spiritualism, gnosticism, philosophical and moral relativism, and a paganism that allowed them in good conscience to indulge themselves in the pleasures of the world. The Corinthian Christians were masters, just as we are in the evangelical church today, at the subtle art of accommodation.

Paul, then, begins with the same bifurcation we experience. How is it possible, he asks, to bring together the "word of the cross" and the "wisdom of the world"? On first reading Paul seems to complicate our dilemma — he admits, even asserts, the quandary of bifurcation: "[The word] of the cross is sheer folly to those on the way to destruction, but to us, who are on the way to salvation, it is the power of God"[1] (1 Corinthians 1:18, NEB). Here is the bifurcation we have been talking about. I proclaim, says Paul, the "word of the cross," and clearly such a concept, such an event and experience, is "sheer folly" to the world. And furthermore, for us as Christians this folly "is the power of God." What a dilemma. Surely this "power of God" is attractive. I want to have a piece of that kind of knowing, knowledge that is the power of God. I want to claim that side of the equation. But must I look foolish to the world? Must I abandon my worldly way of understanding? Must I keep my discipline separate from this dangerously powerful "word of the cross," in order not to look foolish, indeed in order to succeed as a scholar and educator?

Paul is relentless: "Scripture says, 'I will destroy the wisdom of the wise, and bring to nothing the cleverness of the clever.' Where is your wise man now, your man of learning, or your subtle debater — limited, all of them, to this present age? God has made the wisdom of this world look foolish" (1 Corinthians 1:19-20, NEB).[2] Do we find in this strong language an indictment to our calling as educators? In addition:

> God in his wisdom ordained, [that] the world failed to find him
> by its wisdom, and he chose to save those who have faith by the
> folly of the Gospel. Jews call for miracles, Greeks look for wisdom; but we proclaim Christ — yes, Christ nailed to the cross;
> and though this is a stumbling-block to Jews and folly to Greeks,

yet to those who have heard his call, Jews and Greeks alike, he is the power of God and the wisdom of God. Divine folly is wiser than the wisdom of man, and divine weakness stronger than man's strength (1:21-26b, NEB).[3]

Here is Paul's main point: Everything is seen through the cross, through Jesus Christ "nailed to the cross." As we look out across the horizon of the world's knowledge and wisdom, there stands the stark and profound profile of the cross. What are we to make of this troubling and mysterious reality? Folly to the world, the cross stands conspicuously, ominously, indelibly in our way. The cross casts its great, mysterious shadow across the memory of the human race. Our vision, our way of seeing, our view of the world, is marked by the cross. We are destined to think all our thoughts in sight of this profound mystery.

And notice this: If we can grasp this profound notion of the "word of the cross," we claim a promise. God's power and wisdom break open for us. What a claim! What a promise! And yet what folly to the great minds of worldly wisdom. I propose this is not integration of faith and learning. This is not faith seen in the light of my discipline. This is learning, indeed all of life, utterly transformed, standing as we do at the foot of the cross. This is the ground point, the foundation, the lens, the powerfully transforming perspective, through which all knowledge is made new.

We must ask, then, what does it mean to see all things through the "word of the cross"? How are we changed by that great mystery that stands on the horizon of humankind? I admit it might be best not to answer this question. Karl Barth warns us to be careful not to make doctrine out of the cross. It is preeminently an event, both in history and in our own lives. It is the profound mystery we celebrate at the Lord's table. Be careful with explanations. But then it is so difficult to accept this caution. We will follow Paul's lead here and try to explain.

How then does the "word of the cross" define a new kind of learning, redemptive learning? Paul shares with us three important characteristics of learning under the cross. First, standing as we do at the foot of the cross, we confess profound *mystery*. How else can we face the cross, this great reconciling yet inexplicable gift of God's Son, the overwhelming power of God's love and grace, the terrifying recognition of the darkness and brokenness of humankind, the awesome absence and silence of God in the finality of death? Indeed, we must confess mystery.

And just as God stands beyond the cross (the One who calls His Son to inescapable suffering) so we recognize this same God as the Creator and Originator of all life. In the cross this God calls us back into life. The cross is tied to the God of creation, the God of life. The cross is tied to the God of love, undeserved and unconditional love. The cross is tied to the God of history, a God Who will intrude into human space with grace and love, the God of the past and of the future. The cross is tied to the unutterable transcendence of God and yet His profound incarnational presence in human life. Mystery is indeed the starting point with this God. Mystery is the first meaning of the "word of the cross."

While mystery is something we have been trying to eradicate from learning since the Enlightenment, under the cross we stand in awe (and not frustration) that there is much we can know and much we cannot. The cross speaks of surrender. Surely this is what Paul perceived as folly to the Greeks. For the Greeks, human wisdom could most certainly take us beyond mystery to understanding. But as we go about observing the world around us, we know, with Gerard Manley Hopkins, that "the world is charged with the grandeur of God," and just when we think we have it under our control, it will "flame out" when least expected.[4] As Max Weber has said, in our time we have "disenchanted the world." The scientific paradigm under which we still live, inherited as it is from the Greeks, aggressively seeks to dispel any trace of mystery in the process of knowing. What we have lost is wonder, awe, the exhilaration of discovery, expectancy and surprise. These are the things to which this God of mystery calls us in our learning. This is indeed a new kind of learning. This is redeemed learning, reclaimed for thinking Christians.

Humility is the second characteristic of Paul's new kind of learning. The "word of the cross" means that this great God stooped low, very low, and humbly took on the pain and suffering of human life. What kind of God is this? And what kind of learning results? As we stand at the foot of the cross, we recognize human inadequacy and brokenness. We recognize the terrible prospect of human suffering; we recognize pain, darkness and death. Impacted by profound humility hanging there on the cross, we cannot address others or the world with arrogance or self-centeredness. We are servants. We do not assume that our reason, our knowledge or our intelligence are ends in themselves. We simply cannot be manipulative. The Great Servant, the Master of Love, in complete surrender, hangs in this moment, and our lives are transformed. We cannot use our learning but in service to others.

Herein, by the way, lies offense to the Jews, that their Messiah would come as a criminal, a misfit, One who died the worst of public deaths, ridiculed and humiliated by the world. This could not be the hoped-for, triumphant conqueror of the world. To call this Lamb of God, hanging as a sacrifice on the cross, the Messiah was utterly offensive to the Jews, those ever-watchful, messianic hopefuls. What God says to the Jews in this moment is that messianic hope is not national triumphalism. The message should be clear to all of us: Triumphalism of any sort is not the way of the "word of the cross."

The God of a Christ nailed to the cross comes with a different kind of power, not the world's power of wealth or might, but the power of suffering, the power of surrender, and the power of love. It is the last who shall be first in this world of power. This kingdom of the cross is radically different from any kingdom we have ever known. As Jesus hangs there on the cross, God acknowledges profound humility. Knowledge is not power. Knowledge is not control. Paul's new kind of learning, in light of the cross, involves service, love and compassion, a sense of deep humility before our subject matter, a sense of care and concern and love for the world which we study, a sense of compassion and attention for those in need. This new kind of learning makes us servants to our students.

Third, we find *hope* in our new kind of learning under the cross. Jesus Christ mysteriously, miraculously, absorbs our suffering, our brokenness, takes on Himself the great, massive blinding sin of the world, and as He does God's light breaks forth; liberation from brokenness and darkness becomes possible. The "word of the cross" means promise: Resurrection is to come, new life is ahead, the heretofore inescapable bonds of death and suffering are broken. We are reconciled to the God Who stands beyond the cross. We are redeemed, even when we are most irredeemable, to a righteousness that belongs only to God. In the great, dark moment of the cross, the light of the world shines. This cross, then, is ultimately victory, and our new kind of learning must contain this deep sense of promise. Hope is ours. We can study and search, and our answers will be life-giving and full of light.

So Paul presents us with a new kind of learning, learning under the imprint of the cross, and what we find is *mystery, humility* and *hope*. Surely we can agree these three qualities are regarded with ridicule in our own enlightened world. As Paul says, this kind of learning is folly to the world. These qualities do not define the wisdom of this world. The crucial question for Christian educators and thinking Christians is this: When we come to the end of our search, do we find mystery, humility and hope? If so, we have learned under the cross. What a blessed learning this is. What redemption is ours in learning. What a wonderful calling to which we as thinking Christians are called.

We are liberated by this new kind of learning, liberated from the fear that learning will somehow threaten faith: for "a spiritual person can judge the worth of everything" (1 Corinthians 2:5, emphasis added). [5] We find here true academic freedom and a sure sense of the importance of learning. Lest we ever think of Paul as anti-intellectual, that he is afraid of or protective against wide learning, we find here an exuberant, joyous and inclusive view of learning.

"I speak to you," Paul says, "not with 'a wisdom belonging to this present age or to its governing powers, already in decline; I speak God's hidden wisdom, his secret purpose framed from the very beginning to bring us to our destined glory'" (1 Corinthians 2:6-7, paraphrase).[6] The prevailing wisdom of our day is "already in decline." Surely we can agree with the truth of that statement in our own day. But the knowledge *we* seek is "God's hidden wisdom," a "secret purpose." Not only that, but that "hidden wisdom" was framed from the very beginning "to bring us to our destined glory."

As we step into our classrooms, as we open our books of study, as we step into our laboratories to observe the world around, do we really believe that this is our high calling: to bring us, our church and our students to God's destined glory? What more could we ask to define our vocations as Christian educators? If this is the promise for learning under the cross, what more could we seek for the church? This is an end point of spiritual formation.

Paul, then, adds this: "Scripture speaks of 'things beyond our seeing, things beyond our hearing, things beyond our imagining, all prepared by God for those who love him.' ... For the Spirit explores everything, even the depths of God's own nature" (1 Corinthians 2:9-10, paraphrase).[7]

I take this as a ringing endorsement of open and free learning. This is Paul's definition of academic freedom. Informed by the "word of the cross," we can indeed see beyond seeing, hear beyond hearing, imagine beyond imagining. We are equipped to explore everything. As Christians we are not afraid to learn. We are not afraid to explore. We have the ultimate perspective (among all postmodern perspectives) to explore everything, to explore "even the depths of God's own nature." That, by the way, is not an option in our secular institutions of higher learning. Our perspective, through Jesus Christ, emboldens us to explore not only ordinary knowledge of the world around us, but also the nature of God Himself.

Equipped with a new kind of learning, learning with the transforming cross at the center of our perspective, we can find unity in our work. As we all know, unity is not a word held in high regard these days. Diversity, pluralism, relativism, perspectivalism — these are the definers of our day, and all press in the direction of a lack of unity. And to this similar circumstance in the Corinthian world, Paul says, "I appeal to you, [my friends], in the name of our Lord Jesus Christ: agree among yourselves, and avoid divisions; [let there be *complete*] *unity of mind and thought*" (1 Corinthians 1:10, NEB, emphasis added). [8]

To pursue the truth requires that we believe there is some unifying prospect at the end of our pursuits. I am not talking about arrogant, closed claims of the truth, but I am saying, as I think Paul is saying, we can find unity in Jesus Christ.

We live in the world of the multiversity, as Clark Kerr told us some years ago, where knowledge is splintered into disciplines and refined even further into specialties. We are divided into diverse cultures, and in our postmodern times into as many perspectives as there are thinkers.

But we, in the Christian community of higher education, have the chance again to claim the purpose of the uni-versity. We can have unity. We can have our core curricula. We can agree on a canon, the great texts of the world we agree are required reading for any educated person. We can discourse across disciplines. We can come together in civility and mutual respect, across cultures and ethnic backgrounds, across denominational traditions.

I truly believe that when our mission is grounded on the "word of the cross," we can experience genuine community. I further believe, with Mark Schwen and others, that community is at the heart of all good learning. So our Christian colleges and universities can know unity: unity of knowledge, unity of purpose, unity even in love.

One final consequence of learning that is informed by the "word of the cross" is that we are empowered "to overthrow the existing order" (1 Corinthians 1:29ff, NEB). [9] This may sound like the triumphalism humility requires us to dismiss. But in the face of the dominant, highly secular world of learning, our Christian institutions labor under poor institutional self-esteem, not true humility, but a diffidence that takes away courage. We do not really believe we are distinctive or that we are empowered to shape the future of the church or the culture at large.

We look at large public research institutions and measure ourselves against their definitions of quality. We fear we are stuck in the backwaters of higher education, with inferior resources, scholarship that is less than leading-edge, and students who are not among the best.

Paul wants to give us the confidence, complete assurance, that what we have to offer is of ultimate significance. He acknowledges our feelings of inferiority and then affirms the power we have: "He has chosen things without rank or standing in the world, mere nothings, to overthrow the existing order. ... God has made [Jesus Christ] our wisdom, and in him we have our righteousness, our holiness, our liberation" (1 Corinthians 1:28-30, paraphrase). This is so because our teaching, our learning, *"carries conviction by spiritual power"* (1 Corinthians 2:4, emphasis added, NEB). [10]

I truly believe this. We have the chance to be the cutting edge of the next era of higher learning, as of course we were at the beginning of American higher education. Secular institutions have shown us their potential for moral bankruptcy. Most certainly they languish in the confines of a radical political agenda and a strategy of specialization that threatens to render them worthless and irrelevant. The "existing order" is looking for wisdom, for unity, for health and wholeness, and our great universities often squander their right or abandon their desire to speak in these ways.

The "existing order" is looking for answers to dramatic personal and societal problems, and most of higher education shows its cynicism about answers. Answers are "problematic" and "contingent" in the language of current postmodern thought.

How does one live? How does one love? We have discovered that violence and darkness in our cities are in part the result of the breakdown of families. How does one define and commit to healthy marriages and families? How does one know justice? How does one know peace, both personally and corporately? How does one live a life of virtue, integrity and civility?

What is the meaning of the great texts of history, and how does that meaning find application in our lives?

Our kind of learning, "carrying the conviction of spiritual power," a new kind of learning "built not on human wisdom but on the power of God" *can* answer these crucial questions of our day. I think Paul's word here should restore and renew our faith in what we are doing as Christian educators. This is spiritual formation at work among us. And this is the kind of learning that can be the mark of a thriving evangelical church of the future.

My conclusion is this: Informed by Paul's notion of learning through the "word of the cross," we must change our language for the way we address the bifurcation between faith and learning. To talk of integration of faith and learning is too timid, incomplete, in some ways unbiblical. This kind of word, the "word of the cross," is not integrated like some ingredient in the soup of academic life: a pinch of science and a dab of the cross and we have an integrated, scientific Christian soup. No, the cross looms profoundly and decisively in our way. As Christians, we can see nothing except through the great mystery, humility and hope of this event. More than to the notion of integration, Paul calls us to elevated, exalted, redeemed learning. Our call is to transformed minds, the mastery of scholarly tools that see through the trivial, through the surface, tools that see through conventional wisdom of the world to the "secret" wisdom of God.

Some time ago Max DePree changed the metaphor of Christian learning for me. Rather than talk of integration, he said, we must talk about lifting up our learning to our faith. At the foot of the cross we look *up* through Jesus Christ, and we see with transformed eyes. I am absolutely convinced the world waits for us to bring this new kind of learning into its dark confusion. We live in a unique moment in the history of Christian higher education. Education built on the premises of the Enlightenment alone has lost its way: The human mind as the center of all that exists and all that can be known results finally in self-contained emptiness or nihilistic absence. The world and the church desperately need the graduates of our schools who have learned as we learn — at the foot of the cross. We must know what we are doing. We must articulate our case, but as we do, or better yet if we do, the world is watching and listening. What responsibility, what opportunity is ours as Christian educators!

God help us in this awesome task of adopting a new kind of learning at our Christian colleges and universities. God help us as we carry the news of redeemed learning to a world waiting to hear any kind of good news. God help the church to make room for its educators empowered with a new kind of learning. May we all come to affirm that learning is indeed a part of faith, that thinking Christianly is crucial to the credibility of faith in our world. May we come to see that learning is one of the spiritual disciplines, and may we renew our efforts as a people of the cross to a new sense of redeemed learning's power.

ENDNOTES

1. *New English Bible* (New York: Oxford University Press, 1972).
2. Ibid.
3. Ibid.
4. Gerard Manly Hopkins, *Poems and Prose* (New York: Alfred A. Knopf, 1995). Distributed by Random House.
5. *New English Bible.*
6. Paraphrase.
7. Paraphrase.
8. *New English Bible.*
9. Ibid.
10. Paraphrase.

CHAPTER 6
Understanding the Culture of American Higher Education

Steve Moore

My complaint with American higher education is not that there is a values crisis today. It is not a crisis of people's whoring after false gods but that they don't worship at all. Our crisis is the academy's being absorbed in narrow, immediate and ever petty concerns. It is a crisis of apathy, of moral indifference.[1]

At the core of the current dialogue about the future of higher education is a discussion about values. If one turns to any university committee, government agency or governing board in American higher education, one would likely find a discussion in regard to issues of mission, curriculum and core values. Certainly no individual and no institution of higher education can be either officially neutral or unofficially indifferent with respect to value questions without falling into self-contradiction (a state which is certainly not uncommon in higher education). Lloyd Averill correctly points out that any claim to values neutrality is contradictory in part because there can be no community gathered for scholarship apart from the institutionalization of certain values.

> ... Colleges which do attempt, officially or informally, to deny or ignore explicit value questions [i.e. neutrality] are negated in behavior which is dis-integral, if not acutely immoral, since they perpetuate the illusion of neutrality or indifference while actively proceeding to take sides.[2]

One of the early Christian church fathers, Tertullian, asked a pertinent question, one that has been asked again and again in the history of the church and the university: "What does Athens have to do with Jerusalem?" By Athens Tertullian meant the intellectual culture — the life of the mind, and by Jerusalem he meant redemption — the life of the spirit. Throughout the recent history of American higher education a similar tension has existed because of questions relating to the place of values in the educational experience. In Christian higher education this tension has become even more pronounced. Boards, faculty, administrators and others ask, "How do we infuse faith into learning?" or more pointedly, "What is distinctively Christian about Christian higher education?"

Long an institution whose enterprise was characterized as being "dynamic," "evolving" and "democratic," the academy today seems to be at a "wrinkle in time" if not a "major juncture" in the history of its development. In its early stages, American educational pioneers were quite clear of their mission. The Presbyterians, Methodists, Lutherans and others upheld the traditions of the medieval university; it was predictable that their view of higher education included the importance of faith and the Bible, philosophy and reason, as well as an understanding of languages, letters and the humanities. As time went on a certain degree of fragmentation and tension began to be felt. John Henry Newman's words on the task of the university represent the spirit of many a late 19th-century American college's mission or purpose:

> ... to reunite things which were in the beginning joined together by God, and have been put asunder by man ... I wish the intellect to range with the utmost freedom, and religion to enjoy an equal freedom; but what I am stipulating for is that they should be found in one and the same place, and exemplified in the same persons. I want to destroy that diversity of centres, which puts everything into confusion by creating a contrariety of influences. I wish the same spots and the same individuals to be at once oracles of philosophy and shrines of devotion.[3]

As the 19th century passed and the 20th century began, tensions grew more pronounced. The university struggled for an identity separate from the church and grew to be known as a "repository of truth." Higher education grew more embedded in American culture and yet more critical of the culture and its institutions. As the social sciences emerged in the curriculum, the study, and critique, of culture increased. Colleges and universities began to become both a microcosm of the culture conflicts and a lab for problem solving and resolution. To say that the tension has continued to our day would be something of an understatement. As Robert Hariman observes:

> In our own day, it appears that the modern university has become something of a test case for modernity's intertwined commitments to rational inquiry and democratic culture, ... It [the university] is expected to be responsive to a society that is simultaneously becoming more diverse ethnically and more specialized occupationally. It is expected to provide both a forum for cultural differences and the technologies for global modernization ... [it has] been simultaneously defended as the embodiment of modernity's achievements and excoriated as the repository of its vices ... the institution's integrity seems fragile, its purpose unclear, its authority up for grabs.[4]

These difficulties have been further confounded, as Benjamin Barber points out, by the fruits of "modernity" which have served as the foundation of the modern American university. "It has celebrated modernity's victories — emancipation, science, tolerance, reason, pluralism, rights — and it has been diminished by modernity's vices — alienation, deracination, nihilism, meaninglessness, and anomie."[5]

The results in far too many instances appear as numerous observers have described. It is possible — even common — for a student to go to class after class of sociology, economics, psychology, literature, philosophy and the rest, and hardly become aware that she/he is dealing with issues of life and death, of love and solitude, of inner growth and pain.

The student may not even fully grasp the fact that education is not so much information and technique as self-confrontation and change in his or her own conscious life. She/he may sit through lectures and write examinations — and the professors may allow it — collecting verbal "answers," without really thinking through and deciding about any new aspect of his/her own life in any course. Unfortunately, this can be as true at a church-related institution as a public one.

In spite of the current dialogue about "instilling values and ethics" in higher education, some continue to maintain that education should not pretend to make individuals better, only better informed, more efficient or more competent. Ernest Boyer worries out loud about this reductionistic view of learning so present in higher education today when he asks:

> Education for what purpose? Competence to what end? At a
> time in life when values should be shaped and personal priori-
> ties sharply probed, what a tragedy it would be if the most deeply
> felt issues, the most haunting questions, the most creative mo-
> ments were pushed to the fringes of our institutional life. What
> a monumental mistake it would be if students, during the un-
> dergraduate years, remained trapped within the organizational
> grooves and narrow routines to which the academic world some-
> times seems excessively devoted.[6]

In 1990 I began a series of conversations about values with faculty and educational leaders across the United States. My goal was twofold. First, I hoped to identify the values which were informing the work of those influencing higher education's present and future course. Second, I hoped to promote a conversation about matters which often go unspoken in the campus culture. I interviewed men and women from big universities to small colleges, from public institutions to private ones, from rural to urban settings. The conversations were structured within the context of a qualitative research methodology that provided for reflection upon the mission, values and current milieu of American higher education. An initial report of this work is found in my work *The Values of the Academy*.[7] In addition to identifying a set of values most could affirm, the conversations also revealed tension and turbulence around other values, some of which for centuries had been a part of the culture of higher learning.

In her work *Composing a Life* Mary Catherine Bateson examines the lives of five individuals and the ways in which they have shaped, improvised, and otherwise made sense of their "humanness." She describes her study in a manner not unlike how we might describe this study: as an attempt to capture life as "an improvisatory art, about the ways we combine familiar and unfamiliar components in response to new situations, following an underlying grammar and an evolving aesthetic."[8] The metaphors of "an underlying grammar" and "evolving aesthetic" aptly describe the focus of these conversations about the values in the academy, and the attempt to make explicit what are often implicit value affirmations or tensions.

Bateson goes on to suggest that:

> Current research ... often focuses on a single aspect of a stage of life. Dissection is an essential part of scientific method, and it is particularly tempting to disassemble a life composed of odds and ends, to describe the pieces separately. Unfortunately, when this is done the pattern and loving labor in the patchwork is lost ... The recognition [of this] has implications for how the next generation is educated ... [and yet] the American version of the liberal arts education often exemplifies the opposite.[9]

What follows is an attempt to synthesize the values of American higher education into two sets: those values affirmed by most individuals in the academy and those values around which there is considerable tension and disagreement. Combined they help describe the culture of American higher education in its broadest sense, so as not to lose that patchwork and pattern that forms the whole.

Values Affirmations

John Maynard Keynes spoke for the community of scholarship when he wrote, "The power of vested interests is vastly exaggerated when compared to the gradual encroachment of ideas."[10] Repeatedly in our conversations faculty would speak of "ideas" as the soul and identity of the academic enterprise. "We encourage the examination of ideas for the sake of discovering and creating new ideas; it is the most important thing we pass on to our students," stated one faculty member. "The university is here for the mind, not the society," stated another. In addition, faculty were for the most part in agreement that:

> The academy affirms the public nature of ideas; that ideas should be available for public review, scrutiny and testing. Warren Bryan Martin observes that, "Communities of competence" serve as other organizational structures within which public scrutiny takes place. These communities are most often in disciplinary or methodical specializations. However, they serve as a model for the testing and shaping of ideas, not the sole review. Institutions, just as individuals, must have checks and balances against partial vision or error — such scrutiny provides that.[11]

> The academy affirms that "truth" as it is currently "known" is most often partial or fragmentary. It is seen only as "through a glass darkly."

Professor Raphael Demos, of Harvard, is quoted as saying, "Veritas means we are committed to nothing ... for colleges make a commitment to noncommitment ... they demand a perpetual reexamination and have nowhere to rest."[12] While the academy affirms the partial nature of truth, it is at this point that there appears to be an emerging tension, which will be discussed later.

Nonetheless, most would agree that making students aware of the uncertainties of what is known is an obligation of the teacher. Attempting to separate out what is "opinion" and what is "fact" is a never-ending challenge.

> To present as an established truth what is nothing more than an unsubstantiated opinion or a tentative hypothesis is nearly as great a defection from the obligation of a university teacher as it is knowingly to put forward a false proposition as true or to disregard the

existence of available new evidence which throws doubt on what has previously been accepted.[13]

The academy affirms the value of "solidarity" as a manner of making "sense" of the world. It is important at this point to briefly describe what is meant by solidarity as it is used over and against "objectivity."

Richard Rorty has suggested that there are two principal ways in which reflective human beings try, by placing their lives in a larger context, to give sense to their lives.

The first is by telling the story of their contribution to a community. This community may be the actual historical one in which they live, or another actual one, distant in time or place, or a quite imaginary one, consisting perhaps of a dozen heroes and heroines selected from history or fiction or both. The second way is to describe themselves as standing in immediate relation to a nonhuman reality. This relation is immediate in the sense that it does not derive from a relation between such a reality and their tribe, or their nation, or their imagined band of comrades. I shall say that stories of the former kind exemplify the desire for solidarity, and that stories of the latter kind exemplify the desire for objectivity.[14]

Faculty overwhelmingly reported that solidarity is the "way" in which they make sense of their lives, though not necessarily solidarity with other faculty. What is certain is that whether it be family, a cultural group, a small group of colleagues, or an organizing political philosophy (e.g., Marxism), faculty saw solidarity as the primary way in which they made "sense" of things. Nonetheless, most also agreed that, as Ernest Boyer commented:

... there's quite a wide gap between the way they exercise their professional obligations and the kind of lives they live as human beings ... Faculty have solidarity ... but not within academic life; that's not the value of the culture we've built ... solidarity is not what brings rewards.[15]

This value of "solidarity" is also experiencing a certain tension due to the reported sense that the idea of a community of scholars is breaking down as a result of our culture's increasing privatism and a decreasing sense of "common mission" within institutions.

The academy affirms the value of disinterestedness, the willingness to suspend personal or corporate beliefs, "accepted" knowledge, or personal "investment." The academy affirms that this value is required in the pursuit of "truth," new knowledge, new understanding, or new implications from existing ideas.

Central to the value of disinterestedness is the idea of "objectivity," which keeps what is being studied or "known" clearly separate from the student or knower. The desire or motivation is to let ideas stand on their own without the influence of personality, culture, etc. Many observers note that pure objectivity is unrealistic as well as impossible. They believe that the idea of objectivity of itself is far from objective and in fact contaminated by a 19th-century, rationalist, epistemological understanding. Nonetheless, it is a worthy goal, if not obligation, that educators avoid, allowing it to appear that their political or ethical statements are scientific or scholarly statements.

It does not mean or require that educators eschew the assertion of their views or beliefs before their students or the public and speak only of truths agreed upon by the scholarly scientific world, just that they be clear about which are which.

The academy affirms the value of the legitimacy of the exploration and pursuit of ideas without necessarily the knowledge of where that exploration may lead in terms of benefits, conclusions, or outcomes.

If it is not readily apparent, let the point be stated that there is hardly a value affirmed in the academy that is not experiencing a degree of tension! This tension, if not a value, is certainly an expectation. The testing, pushing and evaluating of accepted ideas (i.e., the free pursuit of knowledge), while readily affirmed by faculty, also understandably create tension. However, there appears to remain a conviction among faculty participating in this conversation that knowledge for the sake of knowledge is a worthy pursuit. As one faculty member stated, "Most [academics] are driven by some higher motive to knowledge ... some overriding issue or idea." Or as another faculty person stated, "Intellectual openness or intellectual honesty often means you don't have the end in sight."[16]

Hanna Gray, president of the University of Chicago, affirmed this value in an equally concise manner stating, "The pursuit of learning is itself a value. It does not need to be justified by showing that it has social value and civic virtue, though of course it does."[17]

The academy affirms the value of recognizing the ownership of ideas as expressed and the value of identifying the foundations, roots and connections of ideas.

Several faculty reported the need for increasing the conversations, particularly with students, about the respect and recognition that must be given in regard to others' work. It is a commitment within the university, though sometimes unspoken, that "no one is free to use the distinctive words, ideas, or forms of others without explicit acknowledgment of that derivation."[18] Or as Michael Oakeshott suggests, "The inheritance of human achievements into which the teacher is to initiate his pupil is knowledge ... Knowledge is to be recognized [from whence it came]."[19]

The academy affirms and values the development of that which is aesthetically beautiful, culturally enriching and critically examined.

"In fact, our primary concern is with these intellectual values ... my colleagues in literature would probably say they were concerned with developing student's appreciation of what is aesthetically beautiful ... My colleagues in science ... with a critical and investigative sense ... how the world is put together ... each discipline tends to generate its own value structure."[20]

While the value affirmations might give the appearance of being formalized, highly structured commitments held universally throughout the academy, this study reveals that in a more realistic sense most values are in a somewhat living, dynamic, unpredictable state. It is to those values which most evidently appear to be in transition or tension that we now turn.

The Values in Tension in the Academy

A tension exists in the academy due to the diminishment of the "discourse of civility."

Where disagreement and debate were once appreciated, many educators reported that some colleagues have opted for power "system solutions" where debate, dissent, detraction or opposing views are squelched through the "politicizing" of the discourse. "It's more efficient to get your way to 'process,'" remarked one faculty member. "There are persons," stated Warren Bryan Martin, "who remind us that the characteristics of a community of civility may prove to be more than just another way of trying to maintain the status quo ... [it may be used as] instruments of control, intimidation, and manipulation."[21]

This growing tension is contributed to in part by the tendency among faculty to "form associations around their values ... [and] to gravitate toward those with whom they feel most comfortable." With the values of the academy growing increasingly diverse, the likelihood for tensions increases. Nonetheless, some faculty are hopeful. As a faculty member comments, "I often tell [people outside the academy] that there is a sense of community just being in the same pursuit ... we don't have to agree at all on anything ... I find [that] is what's most exciting about higher education ... [that] you can get very bright, outspoken people just to be around you without having to compromise your position."[22] The tension surrounding the discourse of civility is closely tied to the sense of community in the academy which we will examine next.

A tension exists in the academy due to the declining sense of community among its members.

Increasingly it is difficult to reach agreement on a definition of community or the characteristic features of community in the academy. Some observers point out that this is a phenomenon not unique to the academy, but characteristic of the culture at large. "The university is a microcosm ... a more select microcosm, but a microcosm of our democratic society ... [in which] we lack the vehicles for developing community."[23]

At the core of the academy has traditionally been a commitment to the "community of competence." Those "communities of competence" are most often understood to be the disciplinary and methodological special-izations, including those specializations and methodologies in cognate dis-ciplines. One faculty member suggested that one of the factors contributing to the declining sense of community is the inadequacy of a 19th-century positivist worldview that has contributed to our present understanding of community.

> It is still featured in the way we organize a college. We believe
> that for every genuine question there is a right answer. ... We
> believe that questions which are authentic or genuine are those
> which are compatible. This is neo-Platonism, reinforced by
> Enlightenment, still present on campus today — that all of that
> taken together forms a coherent whole. You can talk about facts,
> and about truth, and feel confident. In those communities of
> competence you'll work that out then and apply it to your disci-
> pline and to your teaching and/or research. So I think there's a
> whole epistemology that functions there. It is being challenged
> by those whose concern is to break down and analyze the com-
> ponent parts. And in so doing, they've concluded that history is
> not steady progression. History is not this legacy of onward and
> upward developments; it's a messy, disjointed process. Suddenly,
> unexpectedly, new paradigms emerge. They also conclude that
> contingencies are every bit as important as continuities.[24]

Perhaps what is yet to emerge is a new paradigm for community. Many are attempting to contribute to a new understanding of community, which in its most basic form consists of at least courtesy and politeness in human exchanges. However, as the Carnegie Foundation has found in its work, many in higher education are skeptical about community.

> I'm kind of skeptical about the whole word. I think the idea of community is sometimes used to paste over the real struggles that are out there that need to be acknowledged. When people talk about community it is frequently a way of trying to get people to conform.[25]

Can the community survive, continue to exist or recast itself in a new form? The challenge of community is one of the central tensions facing the academy today and certainly merits further research and dialogue. However I believe this could be and should be one of the hallmarks of Christian higher education. As community is formed in Christian colleges and universities, it sets a context within which conviction, character and competence can grow and flourish. As Stanley Hauerwas writes, "The story of God does not offer a resolution of life's difficulties, but it offers us something better — an adventure and struggle, for we are possessors of the happy news that God has called people together to live faithfully to the reality that he is the Lord of this world. ... Moreover, through initiation into such a story I learn to regard others and their difference from me as a gift. Only through their existence do I learn what I am, can or should be."[26]

Reflecting on the idea of community, Steve Garber concludes, "... I am more and more convinced that the people you choose to have around you have more to do with how you act upon what you believe than what you read or the ideas that influence you. The influence of ideas has to be there, but the application is something it's very hard to work out by yourself. You work it out in the context of friends ... what does it mean when you're trying to think through new structures or new ways of living, when you don't see models around you?"[27]

A tension exists in the academy due to the phenomena of "political correctness." However, "PC" appears on campuses not as a value or as a "left vs. right" ideological struggle. Rather, it characterizes the *style* of today's debate not necessarily the content; it appears as a symptom, a

metaphor for the tension that occurs most often in relation to curricular or policy debates.

Most faculty agreed that some type of "political correctness" has been a part of the academy throughout its history. From the earliest debates with the church over academic freedom to the loyalty oath of the 1950s, examples of notions of "PCP," politically correct philosophy, were given. As Ernest Boyer remarked:

> The very fact that higher education exists is a value system. There is a fundamental belief that knowledge is better than ignorance! ... Everything [the university] does is value laden ... We haven't examined our own values ... The problem is who decides what values are going to govern and which are disallowed?[28]

Most of the faculty were also in agreement that the current tension is in part related to transitions that took place in the 1960s and 1970s including the entry of faculty who were schooled as students as part of that era. As one faculty member observed:

> In most institutions of higher learning, faculty as well as students and board members came to agree, in the '60s and '70s, to certain politically correct positions ... which were strong actions to correct injustices. ... And to dare to speak against them was to risk alienation and/or ridicule. So the "PCP" notions come right through to the present time. It varies from campus to campus ... i.e. the prevailing social values. If you're not into "gender issues," diversity, multiculturalism, gay/lesbian issues, ethnic/racial issues, radical feminist issues, new age issues ... join in or risk professional scrutiny or redress. ... It's dangerous, now as before, to separate from established thinking [on a lot of campuses].[29]

Others insisted that it was not the diversity itself which was creating the tension of "PCP," but the inability to constructively engage the diversity which created the phenomenon.

... The typical college faculty ... is a congerie of quite diverse and conflicting opinion, and indeed I think the problem of most college faculties is not that there is this press toward conformity of opinion, but that they haven't got the foggiest notion how to make fruitful, creative use out of the diversity that's there. I think part of the privatism of faculty life is that we really don't want to get too close to the diversity that is among us because we're afraid if we do the whole thing will explode. ... The solution on many campuses is not the enforcement of politically correct views, but simply ignoring the whole thing, not dealing with it.[30]

Others suggested that the symptoms of political correctness were attributable to the underlying problem that for many "PCP" had become the modern validation of one's virtue and character in a valueless secular society.

While this may be a comforting psychological response to an age of complexity and ambiguity, it is a disastrous style of discourse of the world of education. Whatever our moral uncertainties, colleges and universities simply cannot function as surrogate religious institutions. Their purpose is to relentlessly challenge beliefs, not to confirm the correctness of personal values or character.[31]

Most faculty were in agreement that the luxury of ignoring the issue of political correctness was one which the academy can no longer afford. Perhaps the attempt to address the symptom of "PCP" and deeper issues associated with it will be the catalyst for the recovery of creation of a new level of discourse in the academy. That faculty have been influenced by the privatism and individualism characteristic of the culture, most faculty would agree. The challenge appears to be in the need for the discovery of new metaphors and models which enable the academy to dialogue about these values. Vartan Gregorian, president of Brown University, remarked in this regard:

The very nature of the academic enterprise necessitates that universities remain partisans of heterodoxy, of a rich and full range of opinions, ideas, and expression. Imposed orthodoxies of all sorts ... are anathema to our enterprise.[32]

A tension exists in the academy due to the introduction of new methods of research and new epistemologies which challenge the traditional "accepted forms of scholarship." The terms "scientific," "historic," "objective," "rational" and "logical" all represent values which are being challenged and tested as there emerges a growing concern that these, or the so-called "empirical" methods, are not always relevant or appropriate in all research.

At the center the concern for objectivity was what others spoke of as "objectivism." It is an understanding of being objective which becomes over-concerned about separation and detachment, both personal and corporate. Ernest Boyer, in speaking to his issue, suggested that the preoccupation with detachment is a rather recent development:

> There is something about the methodology of research, or the kind of worship of rationality that has [become] ... a dominating influence in the academy. There's also something to do with the nature of the language ... We rarely allow ourselves to speak as human beings; that's almost taboo ... The language that is allowed or required is not language that is truly human.[33]

At issue in this conception of objectivity as detachment is a confusion regarding what objectivity demands. Objectivity, many faculty agreed, does require a readiness to accept unpleasant or undesirable findings, but does not require that we do not care what findings may conclude.

Another faculty member added, "A great deal of the problem in the American academy [is] it has never been socially grounded. It has never had solidarity with anything but professionals."[34] Several faculty mentioned structuralism, deconstruction and postmodernism as significant contributors to the development of new understandings. However, the radicalness of these and other movements and their apparent lack of concern with the status quo and the traditions of the academy, faculty find disconcerting. Warren Bryan Martin reflects:

> These people now are coming into the communities of civility

with a disruption ideology. They're not interested in continu-
ity, sequence, order. They're more interested in discontinuities,
in the way science, for example, changes itself abruptly forming new paradigms. They're not interested in Eurocentrism;
they're interested in the new emerging multiculturalism.
They're not interested in cognitive rationality; they like, instead,
insight and inference, they like communal, holistic understanding. ... Now comes the challenge to our way as people emphasize not communities of civility but intentional communities,
confrontational communities, macro communities, communities
of conscience and conviction, and you see them today merging
into curricula. ... There are emerging contending and conten-
tious differences about deep values, about assumptions, about
the basic interpretative framework.[35]

At its best the new breadth of methodologies provides a more clear vision of the world in which we live and the complexities within it.

**A tension exists in the academy due to the issues surround-
ing "the core."**

Because historically the academy has valued competence in terms of a
core of knowledge, there is a significant disagreement over what constitutes "the core" that is to be "transmitted" or "passed" to the next generation. Nonetheless, many faculty were in agreement that:

The canon should be shaped by the necessity of joining worlds
and cultures and should have us learn how to live more fully
and intelligently upon this earth. It should never compromise
those great works which have stood the test of time and generations. At the same time, it should ever be receptive to new voices,
new ways of seeing the world, new visions of humankind, new
directions to global understanding.[36]

However, a tension is also emerging with not just what constitutes "the
core" but challenges the metaphor of "the core." Some faculty felt as if the
end result of "the core" debate would be an academy more clearly focused

on critical thinking skills and the like. Others feared the loss of "the core," as it is now known, undermines the context in which such skills are learned. All seem to agree that whether the core is defined by skills or ideas, the core can be an important symbol of what the college or university values.

A tension exists in the academy due to the ways in which some believe "multiculturalism" has attempted to define the work of the academy.

Still most faculty expressed appreciation for contributions of the "multicultural agenda," particularly to its:

... bringing together of people from diverse cultures and the integration into the whole community and the appreciation and respect for other cultures and people from other cultures, etc. And also, the bringing together of ideas that are multicultural, in other words, books they read, which is simply the working with different ideas and working through different perceptions of the universe and different perceptions of education. Learning how different kinds of people make sense of their lives.[37]

Nonetheless, many faculty expressed personal concern or reported the concerns of their colleagues because of the "fear of being usurped into sort of faddish, superficial commonalties." As well, those faculty suggested, "multiculturalists" often ignore the work of anthropologists, which has deromanticized and dispelled "exoticism that so fascinated and titillated predecessors."

In trying to understand "others" as human beings who cope with concrete problems, often through ingenious strategies, we have come to see them as less mysterious, but more interesting three-dimensional beings of the same human substance as ourselves. Much of the new reverence of diversity, ironically, is based on superficial glimpses that keep the other at arm's length. ...[38]

Questions are asked such as, "Would multiculturalism become the defining criteria by which new research would be evaluated and judged? Would commitments to multiculturalism as understood by outside bodies override the values of institutions and their members?"

Some people wonder if enough attention is being given to the proper limits of diversity. While others are saying this is no time or place to talk about limits. They believe we have not gone nearly far enough ... Let's worry about the consequences later.[39]

Still others believe the idea of multiculturalism to be a value-free concept. It is the problems emerging with the attempts to implement ideas associated with multiculturalism that worries some faculty. Individuals motivated or influenced by political agendas seek to influence the academy's work with little concern for the academy's processes or values. Some believe that:

Multiculturalism's pigeonholing of authors by race and gender is antithetical to humanist tradition. It elevates ignorance and philistinism to a moral principle. No one who has caught even a glimmer of the complexity of Plato and Milton could reduce them to coefficients of race and gender. But students have always sought tools for simplifying the past, for reducing its vastness to a manageable scale. Deconstruction was particularly appealing, because negation always seems more powerful than affirmation. Multiculturalism continues deconstruction's tradition with negation, but cuts a wider swath ... Our public and private language is becoming increasingly inarticulate. When our language shrinks, so does our world. The works of Western civilization offer not just the foundations of liberalism but voices of unparalleled eloquence and beauty. They challenge us to respond. By silencing them we are ultimately silencing ourselves.[40]

Despite such protestations, the sentiment that "if you're not into multiculturalism, a very heavy tide is running against you" was quite strong. On some campuses commitments to multiculturalism were seen as a great achievement, on others a significant liability. Among most faculty it was a tension with an unknown outcome.

A tension exists in the academy due to the conflict regarding the value of "truth seeking" as a historical central mission of higher education.

This tension is confounded by the ambiguity which exists in relation to the relativity of "truth" or the absence of "truth" as an organizational principle. Sheldon Rothblatt describes the situation confronting the academy as one in which:

Today we have gone so far beyond a world of final causes that even the search for truth has an uncomfortable dimension. The extraordinary explosion of information and proliferation of modes of thinking have made it impossible for any one mind to comprehend but a small portion of what is known. In despair the intellect turns back upon itself, creating its own world of rules and looking for reassurance in heuristic models which it is tempted to substitute for reality.[41]

The result of such a situation, some suggest, is that most faculty are uncomfortable, fearing the loss of that with which they feel secure, fearing that the values questions will prove to have no satisfying answers. Additionally, some believe the academy's work is no longer the "search for truth" but merely connecting knowledge or ideas in different ways, "different constructs." For some faculty "truth seeking" is a non-issue:

The only time I ever notice it [faculty talking about the pursuit of truth] is when philosophers talk about scientists doing it. [As a scientist] I always have to say, "What are you talking about?" We're just after an internally consistent descriptive structure that has utility from a predictive point of view. If you have to worry about truth — rather than seek truth now — I'd much rather come back in a thousand years and find out what the current notion of truth happens to be then, because probably very little of anything anybody might say now would have anything to do with it.[42]

For other faculty, the idea of truth seeking is as unnecessary as it is foreign to their understanding of their work world.

> I'm not convinced that there's any particular monopoly that anyone has on the truth ... There are few areas where I'm prepared to say, "well, this is the truth."... [though] I haven't given much thought to that ... [43]

Here again the Christian institution should stand in stark contrast to other institutions because of the organizing center, the person of Jesus Christ. Lesslie Newbigin is especially helpful here when he reminds us, "... [on the one hand] Jesus is the one who subverts 'religion' and contradicts ordinary rationality; on the other, he is the center and the source of all truth."[44]

It is at this point that institutions with missions rooted in the Christian faith can bring two very important distinctives to bear on learning: certainty and humility. While Christian teaching is quite clear that the fullness of truth is known in the person of Jesus Christ, we are also frequently reminded that, "For now we see in a mirror dimly, but then face to face. Now I know in part; then I shall understand fully, even as I have been fully understood."[45]

Most of the great conflicts between the church and the academy have come when the church has insisted upon certainty about matters which have been less than clear in our limited understanding of creation and the world about us. The academy has contributed to the conflicts over "truth" by promoting in spirit and in action an attitude of arrogance which suggests that the first premise of higher learning is to create skepticism, to promote the challenging of all "givens" or assumptions, or to enlighten the naïve and uninformed. Melancthon's admonition that "in essentials unity, in nonessentials liberty, in all things clarity" is a helpful guide.

A tension exists in the academy over the values associated with traditional ways of allocating power and designating leadership.

Conflict is no stranger to the halls of most colleges and universities. Historically, seniority among faculty was understood to entitle one to increasing levels of rank and responsibility. On many campuses at which faculty participating in this dialogue teach, there is a significant amount of growing tension over issues of faculty governance and interaction. "Part of the undercurrent in the political banter that is going on now is that there has been a turn to a kind of an oligarchy ... an intellectual elite which also has happened to have a good deal of the political power," reported one faculty member. Another offered that the traditional ways of allocating power have been challenged by some, while others have attempted to achieve conformity to the "status quo." Nonetheless, "there was a kind of revolt ... the entire tenure committee was tossed out ... there was a dramatic revolution."[46]

Some faculty suggested that a significant factor in the current tension was a "generation gap." Oftentimes faculty who were recruited to institutions a generation ago due to their commitment and loyalty to the school have been replaced by faculty with strong professional credentials. These new faculty hires are sought to improve the academic reputation, yet often come with little or no loyalty to the school. As well they often have little experience in similar institutions and have no sense of the "culture" of small liberal arts colleges.

Without an adequate orientation to the campus ethos, many retiring faculty worry, "Personally, I'm worried about how we will introduce new faculty to the joys of teaching here. ... How do people in this community get to know each other when there are new people who come in so that they have the opportunity to think of working together?"[47]

In addition to tensions emerging among faculty, concerns over power allocation as it relates to administration are also present, as we shall see.

A tension exists in the academy due to values associated with the "corporatizing" of the academy, the reconstituting of the role and function of higher education.

Closely associated with the previous tension is a concern that higher education increasingly views itself as big business. Ideas such as profit-centered management, cost ratios and cost centers, once foreign to the culture of the academy, are becoming more and more a part of the operational ethos of institutions. "I think faculty fear 'them,' you know, the bureaucracy," stated one senior professor. "What I'm thinking of is the faculty resistance to unmitigated, bureaucratic authority ... It often gets couched in terms of issues like free speech and tenure, but it is really about the unrelieved, irrational, entrenched bureaucratic authority which says 'you gotta,' 'you must,' 'you may not.' ..."[48] Some faculty relate the growth and entrenchment of the institutional bureaucracy to the increasing encroachment of governmental agencies. They fear the lack of unity of coherent purpose among faculty provides a natural inroad for control. "The fear of growing (creeping) administrative intervention is a fear of the decoupling of the intellectual and political elites," said a senior faculty member in the liberal arts.

In some cases faculty feel increasingly powerless to slow or halt the perceived "corporatizing" of the academy. This is especially true in institutions which are not heavily endowed and financially secure. As Warren Bryan Martin pragmatically states,

... What they [faculty] probably fear the most is not finding their check in their mailbox on Friday. In other words, we're always very critical of the procedures around an institution, but we always really finally resort to bitter complaints if order isn't maintained ... What faculty fear most depends a bit on their location and sense of security.[49]

A tension exists in the academy over how ideas are valued and how the search for new ideas is rewarded.

Faculty expressed concern over what they sensed to be an increasing spirit of capitalism over ideas in the academy. Some fear that in such a model, "successful," "marketable" ideas will drive out less accepted, less appreciated or less popular ideas — the result being that the academy's role in providing social critique or valuable societal analysis could be undermined.

... There is a tradition in higher education of imagining that you can't really proclaim that truth if you're beholden to the society

... The reality is that the kind of truth seeking the university does is very intimately hooked up with the society, with business and industry, with military, with governmental powers. Everyone knows that there are lots and lots of large universities that would have to close their doors tomorrow if you took away the military-industrial contracts and the big business consulting contracts, and those things obviously drive a certain amount of the generation of knowledge.[50]

And yet there "is an excruciating conflict building up that's damaging to the cherished notion that there can be growth through the tension of differences and to the point of view that in the marketplace of ideas, truth will prevail. It's not guaranteed."

A tension exists in the academy between individualistic and communal modes of learning.

Some faculty suggested that the contemporary American higher education experience is constructed on a system that rewards individualistic, competitive forms of learning antithetical to the communal modes of learning being introduced into our system by other cultural experiences.

In the work *The Good Society*, Robert Bellah attributes to John Locke the current understanding of cultural values in the United States. "It [Locke's teaching] promised an unheard degree of individual freedom, an unlimited opportunity to compete for material well-being, and an unprecedented limitation of the arbitrary powers of government to interfere with individual initiative."

Once detached from its strict Calvinist theological understanding of obligation, Bellah continues, the formation of cultural values was reduced to what could be voluntarily agreed to on the basis of reason.

What has resulted, Bellah concludes, is that societal values have quite simply suffered setbacks in the 20th century with "problems which are ominous in their implications for our future."[51] Abraham Kaplan, on a similar note, flatly states:

Our time is in the grip of what Betrand Russell called subjectivist madness, for which not only values but even facts are thought to be subjectively determined. Over and over the question is raised, Who is to decide — who, rather than how issues are to be decided? The implication is that whether a decision about values, at any rate, is right depending only on how you look at it, which in turn is a matter of who is doing the looking. One person's point of view has as much claim to being right as another's — which is to say, as little claim. There is nothing either good or bad, but thinking makes it so.[52]

Bellah and others have suggested that the modern framework of thinking focuses primarily on the individual and thereby undermines the realizations that institutions, too, have the power and possibility for good and evil.[53] Others have suggested that though the individualistic may be the dominant mode, communal modes of learning are still part of the educational experience.

[The communal] would certainly be part of the historical model of science, for example ... You subject your hypothesis and the way you're testing your hypotheses and the results of the tests to communal discernment, testing. You, to some extent, abide by the conclusions of the community, but sometimes you challenge the conclusions of the community, so there's a communal process of consensus, dissent, new consensus, new dissent ... The other side of the paradox is that there is also a very solitary dimension, I think, to this discernment of truth from falsehood, because there is always the possibility that the community is so wrapped up in its own illusions that the individual needs to go apart into solitude and into receptiveness in order to discern a truth clearly enough to come back to the community and challenge the reigning consensus. So it's a two-way process. We are capable of both insight and deception in solitude; we are likewise capable of both those things in community ... [54]

A tension exists in the academy due to society's expec-

tations which desire more accountability of the academy
and service to society from the academy.

These expectations are in tension with the value the academy places on
being detached from society. "In loco parentis," the concept of colleges
being the substitutionary authority for guiding students' lives, was historically a part of the American higher educational experience until the 1960s
and 1970s when it disappeared from most campuses.

What persisted on many campuses was what might be called "servare
mores de societate," the idea that colleges and universities were responsible, to a degree, for the preservation or transmission of society's values to
the next generation. One might argue that this value was significantly tested
in the 1960s. However, what is most often pointed out is that the 1960s saw
a clash of societal values which were to be "passed on." Some faculty reported that some of their colleagues believe that the university should not
be involved in the transmission of any values, regardless of society's commitments.

> There are some who no longer accept the social and moral di-
> mensions of student learning. Outside of the classroom, they
> reason, they're someone else's job or all on their own. "The
> faculty member's responsibility to students begins and ends in
> the classroom."[55]

Still others observe, "We ought not make the substantive judgment about
what ideas and what values make the most sense or are the most relevant to
the realization of our social goals. Instead, we should seek to develop in
students "analytic capacities," to "teach modes of inquiry" and "to promote opportunities for sequential learning."[56]

However, other educators insist that the academy has a much larger role
which historically has been most identified with institutions of higher learning associated with the church.

> It is only as institutions begin to turn their attention to the total
> educational experience will they begin to achieve the lofty goals
> so eloquently described in their catalogues. It is as we develop

quality learning inside and outside of the classroom and inten-
tionally integrate the two that learning has its greatest impact.[57]
Ernest Boyer adds, a little more emphatically:

Schools and colleges are always in the business of transmitting
values, whether they like it or not, and they are doing it every
moment of every day, in everything they do.[58]

Understanding the Academy: Some Closing Reflections

If one came away from this study believing that, for the first time, change
has invaded our colleges and universities, one would be sadly misguided.
The challenge of change has regularly presented itself to the academy
throughout its history. The question at hand is, can the academy respond to
the current tensions within and without? Will our institutions of higher learning be able to survive (and thrive) in a time when the organizing values of
the academy seem to be unraveling? Robert Bellah offers an important
perspective in that:

... in our life with other people we are engaged continuously,
through words and actions, in creating and re-creating the institutions that make life possible. This process is never neutral
but is always equal and political, since institutions (even such
an intimate institution as the family) live or die by ideas of right
and wrong and conceptions of the good ... [59]

He goes on to suggest that the forming and maintaining of institutions
and our interaction in and with institutions involves calling on models and
metaphors for the rightness and wrongness of our actions and activity. Institutions are not only constraining but also enabling. They are the substantial forms through which we understand our own identity and the
identity of others as we work cooperatively to achieve a decent society.[60]

My experience in conversing with educators from all academy sectors
was encouraging yet sobering. The rapidity, complexity and diversity of
challenges facing higher education seemed both exhilarating and overwhelming to those involved. Faculty, staff, administrators and other educa-

tors involved in these dialogues were eager to wrestle with these substantive issues yet complained about a lack of opportunities or forums to do so. Though faculty held a variety of views on values and their role in the academy, the faculty were eager to discuss both personal and corporate values. Surprisingly, many faculty reported that, much to their disappointment, such conversations about values were rare and infrequent. That a majority of faculty chose solidarity as their means of "making sense of life," but that few found themselves in solidarity with other faculty on their campuses, was both startling and troubling. I was equally troubled and saddened by the tension, solemnness and sense of hopelessness that many individuals expressed about American higher education and its future. As one faculty member remarked, "The academy has lost its sense of humor." I heard similar observations on many campuses, and I have experienced such humorlessness on more than one occasion.

Despite these somewhat discouraging findings, I came away from my conversations encouraged and hopeful. I was encouraged by how deeply committed and devoted most faculty members and other educators are to students and to the purposes of higher learning. As well, I was encouraged by the diversity and richness of ways in which educators were responding to the tensions and challenges presented by the changing world of higher education.

Let me hasten to remind the reader that a majority of faculty participating in the "conversations" of this research worked in public institutions or in private institutions that had no church relation. Nevertheless, even faculty at Christian institutions resonated with the findings. As one faculty member at a church-related college stated, "This is a concise picture of the values I faced in graduate school and the values I encounter with colleagues in my academic discipline from other schools." Another remarked, "I had not stopped to consider that some of the values I picked up in my graduate program may contradict or do a disservice to values I hold because of my faith." Administrators, boards and faculty must realize the challenging and critical task of weighing and challenging values such as these that are a part of the "dominant culture" of higher learning within which Christian higher education exists.

Though the conclusions of this study suggest that there are considerably more tensions in higher education than values that can be affirmed, I believe those tensions provide the grist for higher education's future.

Vaclav Havel, speaking recently of the movement from communism to democracy in Czechoslovakia, described emotions not unlike those described by many within the education enterprise when he stated:

> We realized that the poetry was over and the prose was beginning, that the county fair had ended and everyday reality was back. It was only then that we realized how challenging and in many ways unrewarding was the work that lay ahead of us, how heavy a burden we shouldered. It was as if up to that moment the wild torrent of events had not allowed us to step back and consider whether we were up to the tasks we had undertaken. We had simply been tossed into the current and forced to swim.[61]

He goes on to suggest that:

> Isn't it the moment of most profound doubt that gives birth to new certainties? Perhaps hopelessness is the very soil that nourishes human hope; perhaps one could never find sense in life without first experiencing its absurdity ... [62]

If higher education is to recover its sense of purpose and hope, it will be because of its members' commitment to reclaim the dialogue and discourse which have provided the framework within which the academy's values have been and could be shaped. Albert Camus once suggested that great ideas come "into the world as gently as doves." If we listen attentively, we shall hear, amid the uproar of the confusion of the moment, a faint flutter of wings, the gentle stirring of life and hope. As Warren Bryan Martin has remarked, "Let those who must, despair; let all who will, begin again."

Fifty years ago, Pitirim Sorokin, the founder of the sociology department at Harvard University, released a remarkable book, *The Crisis of Our Age*. In it he predicted that our culture was on a course toward self-destruction. He concluded with the stark offering of one hope, which stands as both a promise and a challenge to church-related higher education faced with the challenges and tensions in contemporary higher education. He closed by saying simply, "*Benedictus qui venit in nomine Domini* ... Blessed is the one who comes in the name of the Lord."[63]

This can and should be Christian higher education's finest moment.

ENDNOTES

1. Abraham Kaplan, "Moral Values in Higher Education," *Moral Values in Higher Education* (Albany, NY: State University Press, 1991).
2. Lloyd Averill, *Learning to be Human: A Vision for the Liberal Arts* (Port Washington, NY: Associated Faculty Press, 1983).
3. John Henry Newman, *The Idea of a University* (New York: Longmans, Green and Company, 1947).
4. Robert Hariman, "The Liberal Matrix," *Journal of Higher Education* 62:4.
5. Ibid.
6. Ernest Boyer, *College: The Undergraduate Experience in America* (New York: Harper & Row, 1987).
7. Steve Moore, *The Values of the Academy* (Ann Arbor: doctoral dissertation, The University of Michigan, 1992).
8. Mary Catherine Bateson, *Composing A Life* (New York: Plume Books, 1990).
9. Ibid.
10. John Maynard Keynes, *Essays in Persuasion* (New York: Norton, 1963).
11. Steve Moore, *The Values of the Academy*.
12. Lloyd Averill, *Learning to be Human: A Vision for the Liberal Arts.*
13. Ibid.
14. Richard Rorty, *Contingency, Irony & Solidarity.* (Cambridge: Cambridge University Press, 1989).
15. Steve Moore, *The Values of the Academy.*
16. Ibid.
17. Hanna Gray, Unpublished address (University of Chicago,1986).
18. Lloyd Averill, *Learning to be Human: A Vision for the Liberal Arts.*
19. Timothy Fuller, ed., *The Voice of Liberal Learning: Michael Oakeshott on Education.* (New Haven: Yale Press, 1989).
20. Steve Moore, *The Values of the Academy.*
21. Ibid.
22. Ibid.
23. Ibid.
24. Ibid.
25. Ibid.
26. Stanley Hauerwas, *The Community of Character: Toward a Constructive Christian Social Ethic* (Notre Dame, Indiana: University of Notre Dame Press, 1991) 148-49.
27. Steve Garber, *The Fabric of Faithfulness* (Downers Grove: Inter Varsity Press, 1996).
28. Steve Moore, *The Values of the Academy.*
29. Ibid.
30. Ibid.

31. Paul Schulman, "Political Precepts Tied to Personal Identity," *Chronicle of Higher Education*, (8 January 1992).
32. Vartan Gregorian, "The Many Faces of Political Correctness," *Educational Record* (Winter 1992).
33. Steve Moore, *The Values of the Academy*.
34. Ibid.
35. Ibid.
36. Huel Perkins, "The Canon and New Voices," *Chronicle of Higher Education* (19 February 1992).
37. Steve Moore, *The Values of the Academy*.
38. Richard Perry, "Why do Multiculturalists Ignore Anthropologists?" *Chronicle of Higher Education* (4 March 1992).
39. Steve Moore, *The Values of the Academy*.
40. Heather MacDonald, "Multiculturalism Triumphant," *The New Criterion* (January 1992).
41. Sheldon Rothblatt, *Tradition and Change* (London: Faber and Faber, 1976).
42. Steve Moore, *The Values of the Academy*.
43. Ibid.
44. Lesslie Newbigin, *Foolishness to the Greeks* (Grand Rapids: Eerdmans, 1986).
45. Holy Bible, *Revised Standard Version*, 1 Corinthians 13:12 (Nashville: Thomas Nelson Inc., 1971).
46. Steve Moore, *The Values of the Academy* (Ann Arbor: doctoral dissertation, The University of Michigan, 1992).
47. Ibid.
48. Ibid.
49. Ibid.
50. Ibid.
51. Robert Bellah, *The Good Society* (New York: Knopf, 1991). Distributed by Random House.
52. Abraham Kaplan, "Moral Values in Higher Education."
53. Robert Bellah, *The Good Society*.
54. Steve Moore, *The Values of the Academy*.
55. Ibid.
56. Ibid.
57. Alexander Astin, "The Challenges of Higher Education." Unpublished address, The Puget Sound Student Affairs Colloquium (February 1995).
58. Steve Moore, *The Values of the Academy*.
59. Robert Bellah, *The Good Society*.
60. Ibid.
61. Paul Wilson, *Open Letters: Selected Writings 1965-1990 of Vaclav Havel*

(New York: Knopf, 1991). Distributed by Random House.
62. Ibid.
63. Pitirin Sorokin, *The Crisis of Our Age* (New York: Dutton Press, 1992).

CHAPTER 7
Getting It Together: The Role of Cultural Diversity in a Christian University

Richard T. Hughes

There was a time, early in my teaching career, when I thought the phrase "Christian university" was in many ways an oxymoron, a virtual contradiction in terms. That belief grew from a whole variety of accumulated experiences, ranging from my undergraduate years in a southern, church-related college in the early 1960s, to my graduate studies at a state university in the late 1960s, and finally to my experience as a young professor at Pepperdine University in the early 1970s. I no longer hold that viewpoint.

Nonetheless, I want to share with you my story so that you can understand why I drew those conclusions. Finally, I want briefly to explain why I now feel that "Christian" and "university" can be — and should be — mutually reinforcing ideals.

Cultural Diversity and Academic Rigor

I arrived at Pepperdine University in 1972 as a raw recruit, only 28 years old and the youngest faculty member. Not only that, I arrived in many respects as a child of the 1960s. In many ways, this seems strange to say, for I never really encountered the 1960s until that decade was almost over. In 1967, I enrolled in the religion school at the University of Iowa where the pressing issues of racism, civil rights and the war in Indochina suddenly became my daily bread. I could not have escaped those debates, even had I tried. My professors raised them. My fellow students raised them. The entire university community, in fact, was awash in those years in a sea of ethical and moral passion. This was not unique to Iowa, since these issues burst into life with almost terrifying intensity on the campuses of most American colleges and universities at the time.

There were critics of American universities in those years who claimed that the campus unrest, protests and debates served only to undermine and disrupt the educational process. In my experience, just the reverse was true. The university climate in those days virtually dictated that one could *not* rest content with comforting orthodoxies and narrow, provincial assumptions, for the world had come to the university, and it was the world of cultural pluralism. It was a world of African-Americans and Asians; Hispanics and Native Americans; Buddhists and Hindus; Moslems and Jews. It was a larger world than I had ever known before, and my professors and peers demanded that I take it seriously.

That requirement turned out to be a fundamental part of my graduate education, for it forced me to think and to ask questions I had never asked before. I raised questions about my faith: How did I know that my beliefs were true? And if they were, which of my beliefs were merely products of culture, and which were timeless? And there were questions about my own cultural background. I had grown up in west Texas assuming that my own experience as a white, middle-class American was the standard by which all other cultures should be measured. I never thought much about that assumption. I came by it naturally since, in my own limited experience, nothing had ever caused me to question it. There were African-Americans and Hispanics in my high school, but our worlds seldom touched. Instead, I moved in a circle of friends who were essentially like me: white, Anglo-Saxon and Protestant. The truth is, I knew so little about other cultures that I never took them seriously.

Suddenly, all that changed. Now, as a student in a large, multicultural university in the midst of the social upheavals of the 1960s, the easy cultural assumptions of my youth simply evaporated and disappeared. I remember well one particular instance when this occurred. I was serving as a teaching assistant in a large, undergraduate course titled Religion and Culture. One of the books we used in that course was the *Autobiography of Malcolm X*, and it exerted an enormous impact on my thinking. For the first time, I caught a glimpse — a very small glimpse, to be sure — of what it meant to be black in America's urban ghettoes. For the first time, I saw ways in which I had been insensitive to cultures not my own. I now began to see why Malcolm viewed whites as devils, and why he finally turned his back on Christianity as a tool of white oppressors. And I saw why Malcolm found Islam so attractive. Suddenly, Malcolm X had shattered my world of easy assumptions and simple answers. Somehow, I had to piece it back together again.

At this point, my professors came to my aid. They never gave me easy answers. They did, however, ask me to read, and to read widely. They asked me to think, and to think systematically. And they asked me to discipline my thinking through writing. In a word, they imposed on me a level of academic rigor I had never known before.

As an undergraduate, I thought of academic rigor mainly in terms of knowledge: in terms of the facts I had mastered, or of vast amounts of data that I had memorized and now could spit back on exams. Now I was exposed to a whole new dimension of academic rigor. Quite simply, it involved thinking and systematically reflecting on historical, ethical, religious and philosophical problems.

I well remember taking a major qualifying examination in the area of theology. I had two shots at this exam. I could flunk it once and remain in the program; flunk it twice, and I was out. I prepared hard for that exam. I memorized the salient points of many of the great theologians: Augustine, Aquinas, Luther, Barth, Tillich and others. I knew the material well. I had no doubt that I would ace this exam.

But when the professor returned my paper, he had placed on the front a large, red "F." Stunned and dismayed, I paid him a visit. "I don't want you to memorize the thinking of the great theologians," he said. "I want you to theologize. I don't want you to regurgitate the thinking of others. I want you to use their thinking in creative ways, and then to think for yourself." I went back to the drawing boards and managed to pass the exam the second time around.

I found this business of thinking for myself to be very hard work. It involved in-depth reading and systematic understanding. It involved analysis and assessment and careful comparison of multiple traditions and perspectives. It involved asking hard questions about the influence of history and culture and the relation between culture and religion. And in the process, it demanded intellectual honesty, even when that honesty threatened earlier beliefs, assumptions and prejudices.

Though it was tough, I finally embraced this method. It was the only way I knew to answer the questions which had now become for me so urgent and pressing. In the first place, the answers to my questions had to be my own, not answers I had inherited from parents, teachers or friends. Further, as I think on it now, I realize to what an enormous extent the academic rigor I was forced to employ grew directly from the cultural diversity that had invaded my world. After all, if one's world is single-dimensional, if one's worldview is defined by orthodoxies that are never challenged, then one hardly has to reflect, explore, think or examine at all. One only has to affirm and defend. But if one's world is multidimensional and complex, if one takes seriously a variety of worldviews and a variety of perspectives that differ from one's own, if one seeks to understand other traditions, other religions and other cultures, then one really has no option other than rigorous and systematic analysis. For this reason, I finally came to see that cultural diversity and academic rigor comprise the very essence of any university worthy of the name.

Cultural Diversity and the Christian Life

During those years, I made another discovery about the value of cultural diversity. I learned that if it is fundamental to rigorous academic investigation, it is also fundamental to the Christian's moral and spiritual life. Perhaps I can best explain the point I seek to make by citing the words of Jesus in the Sermon on the Mount.

"You have heard that it was said, 'Love your neighbor and hate your enemy.' But I tell you: Love your enemies and pray for those who persecute you, that you may be sons of your Father in heaven. ... If you love those who love you, what reward will you get? Are not even the tax collectors doing that? And if you greet only your brothers, what are you doing more than others? Do not even pagans do that? Be perfect, therefore, as your heavenly Father is perfect" (Matthew 5:43-48).

If perfection meant that we should extend our love and concern to people beyond our own circle, then I was far from perfect. I had spent my entire life associating with people like myself: whites, Southerners, Anglo-Saxons, members of the Church of Christ. All those categories were important to me, but the one that defined the parameters of my life more than any other was the Church of Christ. As a child and adolescent, my entire being revolved around this church. Further, since we believed that ours was the one true church, there seemed little reason to associate with people of other religious traditions and, for the most part, we didn't.

In high school, I expanded my horizons. But not far. I now had close friends who were Methodists and Baptists, and even a few who were Presbyterians. While we engaged in vigorous religious debates, culturally we were all the same: white, Anglo-Saxon, middle-class, Protestant.

When I finally got to college, nothing really changed except that, from a religious point of view, my world grew even smaller. There, 99 percent of the students and 100 percent of the faculty belonged to that same church. No one ever suggested that I should expand my religious horizons, and I was content to be among my own.

Then I went to Iowa. In many respects, Iowa was not far from my home — less than a thousand miles, almost due north. But in other respects, it was a million miles away. The first thing I learned about Iowans was, they talked funny. We hadn't been in Iowa City more than a day or two when we had to tank up with gas. Those were the days of "full service." When the attendant approached my window, I told him, in my normal Texas drawl, to "fill it with reglar" and "check the all." The attendant, who spoke like all Iowans — in good, standard, radio speech — promptly replied, "I will, sir. But all the what?" Exasperated, I repeated, "Check the *all*." "Yes sir," replied the attendant, "but all the what?" I couldn't believe that one person could be so dense. "The *all*," I screamed. "The *all*." "Yes sir," he said, "but all the what?" "Check under the hood," I finally muttered in defeat.

When I got home, I told my wife, Jan, who was from Chicago, about my experience with Iowans who didn't know how to talk. She had a different assessment. She told me that I was the one who didn't know how to talk. She said she would work with me, and she did. Every night. "Oil," she said. "All," I responded. Slowly, I improved. "Oil," she said. "Oiyal," I repeated. Finally, in the interest of preserving my self-respect, I quit saying the word altogether.

I soon discovered that my Texas drawl would be the least of my problems in Iowa. The far greater challenge would be what struck me as an extraordinary level of cultural and religious diversity. I had grown up with Smiths, Joneses, Robbins, Parks and Wilsons. Now I found Schwartzendrubers, Gingriches, Yoders, Bettenhausens and Spriestersbachs. This, I soon learned, was a region populated by Germans, Norwegians, Czechs and Danes.

Churches of Christ in most Iowa towns ran from minuscule to nonexistent. Southern Baptists, whose churches boasted hundreds and thousands of members throughout my native Texas, didn't fare much better. There was one Southern Baptist church in Iowa City, and it had all of 60 members.

On the other hand, Catholics and Lutherans were everywhere. They dominated the cities, the towns and rural countryside. I found Methodists and Presbyterians, to be sure, but I also found Mennonites and Amish and Quakers — Christian traditions with which I had absolutely no previous acquaintance.

Before I went to Iowa, well-meaning friends — mainly much older than myself — had warned me not to go there at all. They claimed I would lose my faith, studying religion in a godless state university dominated by liberals at best, and by infidels and atheists at worst.

I found in Iowa's School of Religion, however, a very diverse community of serious believers. I did have friends among the graduate students who belonged to the Church of Christ, but aside from them, my two best friends were Catholic and Mennonite. My professors were Jewish, Buddhist, Catholic, Lutheran, Unitarian and Presbyterian.

Not only did I not lose my faith, I found my faith challenged in ways it had never been challenged before. Further, that challenge had everything to do with cultural diversity. It occurred as I saw manifested in the lives of my colleagues and professors compassion and concern for the suffering and oppressed of widely diverse cultural backgrounds, both in America and throughout the world. And it occurred especially in the context of America's struggle over civil rights and the war in Vietnam.

I am aware that there were many in the 1960s who used the turmoil of that period as an excuse to rebel against traditional values. This was not the case, however, for my professors and most of my university colleagues and friends. For them, the social and ethical issues of that period were deeply religious issues, and their personal feelings about the war and their strong support for civil rights and basic equality for all Americans grew directly from their religious convictions.

While I knew full well that there were Christians who stood on both sides of the Vietnam War question, I found myself deeply impressed by professors and friends who refused to support that war, who resisted the destruction of a culture different from their own, and who grounded their resistance in the words of Jesus, "You have heard that it was said, 'Love your neighbor and hate your enemy.' But I tell you: Love your enemies and pray for those who persecute you, that you may be sons of your Father in heaven." I was equally impressed by my colleagues among the graduate students especially, who stood with blacks in very concrete ways in the struggle for equal rights and opportunities.

In a word, I learned at Iowa that cultural diversity involves not only race and ethnicity, but also economic and social standing, and that cultural diversity ministers not only to the life of the mind, but also to the moral sense and to the life of the spirit.

Further, as I thought on these things, it struck me that concern for cultural diversity — for the foreigner and the stranger in our midst — stands at the very heart of the Christian witness. One need only recall the life and deeds of Jesus Who befriended the Samaritan woman at the well; Who forgave the woman taken in adultery — the woman all the others called unclean; Who visited the house of the tax-collector, Zacchaeus, over the protests of the people who complained, "He has gone to be the guest of a 'sinner'"; and Who finally offered forgiveness to the thief on the cross. Cultural diversity, in a word, is a distinctly Christian virtue, for it simply means that we prize those who differ from ourselves.

The Harding College Years

As I reflect on those years, I now find it curious that I finally discovered the value of cultural diversity at a state university, not at the Christian college I attended in the early 1960s. Harding College was located in the South where America experienced the opening phase of its greatest revolution since the Civil War. Yet, this revolution passed me by. Somehow, in spite of my geographical proximity to these events, I managed to remain blissfully unaware of these struggles. The lunch-counter sit-ins in Nashville and Greensboro, the march on Selma, and the brutal repression of black children in Birmingham in the summer of 1963 — all these events simply passed me by like a train in the night. Not until I reached Iowa City in 1967 did I finally discover the 1960s and the great moral and spiritual lessons that decade had to teach.

Now, at age 50, I stare in amazement and disbelief at the documentary film *Eyes on the Prize*, which depicts so powerfully the black struggle for civil rights during that period. I am astonished when I see blacks and whites, no older than I was at that time, traveling on interstate buses throughout the South, challenging the longstanding southern laws that forced blacks to sit in the back and whites in the front. I watch as thugs in Birmingham, AL, beat the students unmercifully when they disembark the bus, and then I hear one of the students tell from his hospital room that he will continue to fight for the rights of the poor and the oppressed, even if it costs him his life.

As I watch this film, I cannot help but recall the words Jesus spoke in the synagogue of His own hometown when He proclaimed His task and mission.

"The Spirit of the Lord is on me,
> because he has anointed me
> to preach good news to the poor.
He has sent me to proclaim freedom
> for the prisoners
and recovery of sight
> for the blind,
to release the oppressed,
> to proclaim the year of the Lord's favor" (Luke 4:18-20).

All these things happened in 1961, the year I was a freshman in college. I stare in disbelief, not only because these students displayed such incredible moral courage, but also because I was so completely unaware of these events when they occurred, even though I was living and studying no more than 500 miles away.

I place another film in the VCR. This time, white thugs have just murdered Mississippi's black political leader, Medgar Evers. Now, students from colleges and universities throughout the United States pour into Mississippi to help inform rural blacks regarding their opportunities and to help break the stranglehold which the White Citizens' Council now has on the state. This time, three young students — all of them my contemporaries — are murdered, literally giving their lives for those of a different culture who have neither power, wealth, nor ability to repay their efforts.

I do not fully know why I missed the impact of those events at the time they occurred. In part, I'm sure I was neither watching nor listening, preoccupied as I was with grades, dating and a host of other matters that some-how seemed more urgent. At the same time, the administration and faculty — at least in my experience — seldom if ever portrayed the civil rights revolution in a favorable light or brought the dramatic events of those years to the students' attention in a positive way.

In spite of all that, Harding College was a profoundly Christian place in many respects. Most of all, it provided its students with a rich spiritual heritage. It nurtured the wellsprings of the heart and taught us the value of worship and praise. It focused our attention on a sovereign God and taught me, for the first time in my life, what it meant to be justified by grace through faith. Simply put, if I learned at Iowa the public and ethical impli-cations of the gospel, I learned as an undergraduate the more private, spiri-tual and devotional side of the Christian faith.

The Pepperdine Experience

Then, in the fall of 1971, I joined the faculty at George Pepperdine College, as it was then called, located in South Central Los Angeles, at the corner of Vermont and 79th. Even then, Pepperdine was a curious kind of institution. It was related to the Churches of Christ, but it was nothing like Harding. In the first place, it was profoundly multicultural, with significant ethnic and economic diversity. In the second place, it enrolled a relatively small number of students who belonged to Churches of Christ, and a large number of students who didn't claim the Christian faith at all. In many respects, it seemed more like Iowa than Harding, more like a state univer-sity than a Christian college. Having just come from Iowa, I felt very much at home. Yet, Pepperdine also had a profoundly Christian core, both in the faculty and among the students, comprised of members of Churches of Christ as well as people of other Christian traditions.

Then in 1972, Pepperdine opened its new campus in Malibu. Though that campus created great excitement among virtually all concerned, those were extremely difficult years. They were difficult especially because a vast, ideological chasm now ran through the heart of the faculty, dividing it virtually down the middle. The division played itself out over the single issue that had polarized all America for almost 20 years — the issue of cultural diversity.

In many ways, the new Malibu campus provoked the rupture since it symbolized new beginnings and therefore occasioned such radically different visions of what Pepperdine at Malibu should finally become. On the one hand, many faculty, especially the older faculty, had come to Pepperdine from traditional, Church of Christ-related colleges like Harding in the late 1950s and early 1960s. They nurtured a vision of a school that would especially serve the Churches of Christ, a school that would promote the heritage of Churches of Christ, and that would instill in students the more private, spiritual values of the Christian religion. They wanted to recruit faculty from Churches of Christ and students from Churches of Christ, and to make Pepperdine at Malibu a definitive, new institution, serving especially this tradition.

On the other hand, many younger faculty were essentially products of the 1960s, had experienced the cultural diversity of that period at various major universities throughout the country, and had thrilled to the academic rigor which that diversity had promoted. Further, these faculty celebrated multiculturalism as a virtue clearly in keeping with the highest calling of the Christian faith. They therefore resisted efforts on the part of the older faculty to make Pepperdine more like Harding or one of the other, more traditional Church of Christ-related colleges.

Older faculty often viewed younger faculty as radicals, hotheads, and subversive of the college's mission. Younger faculty, for their part, often saw the older, more traditional faculty as sticks-in-the-mud and barriers to Pepperdine's development as a culturally diverse and academically rigorous institution.

Little wonder, then, that I — along with many other younger faculty of that period — finally came to see the phrase, "Christian university," as an oxymoron, a contradiction in terms. It seemed to us that many among the older faculty wanted to build a church, not a university. And it seemed to many of the older faculty that their younger colleagues wanted to build an academically sound university with no distinctly Christian underpinnings.

Conclusion

Now, almost 20 years later, I reflect on the turmoil of those days with considerable sadness. The polarization that occurred not only divided the Pepperdine community in needless and unproductive ways; it also split apart two commitments that should have reinforced one another: the Christian commitment and the commitment to cultural diversity.

On the one hand, a Christian university must nurture Christian commitment at all levels of the institution, and must allow that commitment to shape classroom instruction, the curriculum and the university at large. Apart from this dimension, a university can hardly claim the name "Christian" at all.

At the same time, a Christian university must actively prize and cultivate cultural and even religious diversity. In the first place, diversity stands at the heart of the academic enterprise and helps sustain the life of the mind. In fact, without a healthy dose of diversity, there can be no university at all. But in the second place, cultural diversity is a distinctly Christian virtue without which any Christian university would be greatly impoverished. This means that a seriously Christian university should never merely tolerate a diversity of people and ideas, but should embrace them and welcome them as indispensable allies and friends. It should do so not because it seeks to be politically correct, but because it seeks to be faithful to the example of Jesus Christ Who took seriously all men and women of all races, religions and cultural backgrounds.

Historically, it has not been easy to sustain a university that is distinctly Christian and distinctly diverse at one and the same time. This is because Christianity is finally a particularistic religion, and many Christian institutions of higher learning have had great difficulty reconciling the particularistic dimensions of the Christian faith with the diversity that characterizes the university.

Yet, the genius of the Christian faith lies in the universality of its own particularity. It centers on a God Who "so loved the world," and on a Person Who gave Himself for all humanity. Precisely here, at the center of the Christian faith, one finds the only foundation for the serious integration of the two most important commitments of the Christian university: the commitment to the Christian faith and the commitment to serious exploration of the culturally diverse world in which we live.

CHAPTER 8
Struggling to Manifest the Sacred

Robert Wuthnow

There are three questions which must be answered as one considers the future of church-related higher education. First, how are the resources on which church-related higher education depends changing? Second, how do church-related colleges manifest the sacred? And third, what are their prospects for the future?[1]

As I begin to attempt to answer these questions let me reveal a few of my assumptions.

One is the impossibility of predicting the future (much as we would like to). It is for that reason that my comments will be pitched at a somewhat higher level of abstraction than might normally be considered "user friendly." I do this simply because one has to focus more on the kinds of issues ("variable," if you will) that may be important, rather than specific episodes and events.

A second key assumption is that inceptions such as colleges and universities depend on resources. Who would disagree? The point, though, is that these resources also influence the shape (not simply the strength) of those institutions. And a secondary point is that resources have paradoxical, or at least ambiguous consequences — meaning that it is all the more important to be modest in thinking about the future. In relating church-related institutions to their resources, I will actually be drawing from some of my previous work in which I have developed a "population ecology" approach to the study of religion. For our purposes, we can dispense with most of the technicalities of this literature, however, and move to the substance of the issues at hand.

Finally, I want to signal at the outset that I do not necessarily equate "church-related" with "religion" or "manifestations of the sacred." That relation is also more complex, in my view, than many observers have suggested. Thus, I take issue with those who emphasize the inexorable processes of secularization in dealing with church-related higher education. My argument on that score is similar to the one I proposed in my book *The Restructuring of American Religion.*[2] There I also denied the value of thinking about secularization in linear terms. Instead, I suggested that a major realignment has been taking place in American religion with a shifting away from denominational loyalties toward a new division between religious liberals and religious conservatives.

That division is certainly relevant for the understanding of higher education as well, especially because many church-related colleges are on the conservative side, while many secular colleges contribute to the liberal side. To suggest that there is some unsolvable "culture war" going on is, however, mistaken. Church-related colleges are for the most part a force in the middle. They include not only conservative, but also liberal — and even secular — tendencies. And public universities are not only secular, or liberal, but contexts in which the sacred is evident as well.

So, without any further ado, let me turn to the first of my three questions: How are the resources on which church-related colleges depend changing?

The resources that give Christian higher education the opportunity to manifest the sacred fall into two categories: those that contribute to the general goals of colleges and universities, and those that affect the specific place of religion within these organizations. The former have for the most part been on the increase over the past century or more, while the latter have shown a mixed pattern.

The overall work of colleges and universities depends greatly on the presence in virtually all modernized societies — and in most developing societies as well — of a value structure that legitimates higher education. So pervasive is this legitimacy, in fact, that its significance can easily be overlooked. Yet it is inconceivable to think of middle-class parents saving as seriously as they do for anything else, with the exception of their homes, as to pay for their children's college educations. To say that colleges and universities depend on a favorable value structure is thus to suggest something more than a subjective predisposition to recognize the importance of higher education. These values take on objective stature in the budgets of families and state administrators. They are also a pervasive aspect of the public culture, manifested in the mass media and history books as well. Children grow up knowing that higher education is an integral feature of the adult world much in the same way they probably knew that about the church in medieval societies.

Values are nevertheless of little significance in this case except for the fact that in modern societies such as the United States there is also the economic wherewithal to make good on these values. The fact that middle-class parents can afford to pay amounts equivalent to a quarter or more of their family incomes for annual college tuition payments is evidence of the margin for discretionary expenditures that exists in these societies. Affluence is one of the environmental conditions on which the current system of colleges and universities greatly depends.

The economy is, however, more integrally related to higher education than simply being a source of external support. Higher education is generally thought to feed resources back into the economy, and this relation is so complex that secondary systems of reward and social status have also become closely linked with the attainment of advanced education. Part of what legitimates vast social expenditures on higher education is the assumption that these funds actually constitute an investment in the future, an expense that will reap high dividends, both for the society at large and for the individuals directly involved. Higher education is justified in utilitarian cost-benefit analyses in ways that expense on, say, religious institutions seldom can be. In addition, higher education has become a major determinant of social status and of the numerous lifestyle differences associated with the stratification system. Entry into various occupations is heavily contingent on having attained the appropriate educational credentials, a fact that becomes all the more significant when other criteria, including ethnic origins and "creeds," have been made illegitimate in most societies. Even on such private matters as choice of marital partners, similar educational levels have risen in importance relative to such traditional criteria as national, regional and religious homophily.

All these broader conditions would still be of little importance were it not for the organizational resources that have been amassed over the decades by colleges and universities themselves. These include the evolution of the professorate as a legitimate occupational choice, the gradual development of a significant segment of the labor force trained to occupy positions within the professorate, methods of certifying the professional status of — and of restricting entry into — these positions, a relatively stable system of rankings, division of knowledge into academic disciplines, and the organization of colleges and universities into schools and departments. These organizational resources are largely taken for granted on a day-to-day basis, yet many of them scarcely existed a century ago, and many are still subject to ongoing discussion and modification at colleges and universities around the country.

A review of the resources on which colleges and universities depend would also be incomplete if it failed to mention the role of the state. On the surface it is obvious that a large share of the funding for higher education now comes from public sources. But the state is a critical factor in orchestrating a favorable climate for higher education more generally. Just as Max Weber pointed out in tracing the conditions favorable to the rise of capitalism in the West, so we might emphasize that long-term political stability has been a significant element in the development of higher education. Regimes that have tried to control higher education too closely or intimidated scholars to the point of causing them to emigrate, or even regimes that led their populations into costly and destructive wars, have contributed negatively to the evolution of colleges and universities. These examples also attest to the importance of political and legal respect for traditions of academic freedom, not to mention the positive encouragement given to higher education by politically motivated competition between states and foreign powers or between political units within the same national arena. The current competition between the United States and Japan to support effective systems of higher education has a long precedent in similar competitions between France and Germany in the 19th century or between Scottish and Dutch universities at an earlier date. Even the competition between universities such as Ohio State and Indiana University is rooted in political division and has consequences quite similar to those that resulted in the growth of a national system of universities within the German territories in the last century.

Finally, it is worth mentioning the broader system of supportive organizations on which colleges and universities depend. Like any business firm, no college or university exists in a vacuum, but carries out its activities in connection with numerous subcontractors and supplemental organizations. These include national testing organizations, without which the complex decisions surrounding recruitment and selection of students would be impossible; the professional associations to which faculty members belong; publishing companies that produce textbooks; insurance companies; alumni groups; the military; and hosts of other academic suppliers.

All these resources contribute to the overall prominence of higher education in modern societies. Without these resources, colleges and universities would be unable to carry out their stated educational aims and would have a smaller impact on the public sphere more generally. To this degree, a reduction in many of these resources might also affect the likelihood of colleges and universities being able to infuse ideas about religion into the public arena as well. That likelihood, however, also depends on some resources concerned more specifically with the role of religion in higher education. Some of the resources — for example, the overall strength of denominational hierarchies capable of supplying financial support to church-related colleges, or a political system that respects the right of religious organizations to operate in the educational sphere — are relatively straightforward, but the role of others is sometimes counterintuitive.

One example of this kind of resource is the role played by the First Amendment to the United States' Constitution in encouraging or discouraging religion within American higher education. It has been argued that separation of church and state has worked to the disadvantage of religion in higher education because public monies were thereby denied to organizations advancing the cause of religion. It has also been argued, however, that such separation played a positive role in that it prevented government from restricting religious activities and encouraged voluntary contributions to religion in higher education, just as it did to the churches more generally. Contradictory as these two arguments may seem, the truth is that both are probably correct. Indeed, it has probably been the combination of circumstances suggested by both arguments that contributed most to the present state of religion in American higher education.

Separation of church and state has often posed a challenge for church-related colleges or for those wishing to include religious offerings on secular campuses. It presented enough of a challenge to encourage voluntary support for private church-related colleges draconian in its execution. Government officials have for the most part taken a loose interpretation of the First Amendment, permitting public monies to be granted to church-related colleges for, say, the building of dormitories, or the support of individual students under the National Defense Education Act, or the sponsorship of scientific research at church-related colleges. What is probably of greatest significance is the fact that the relation between church and state was thus fraught with uncertainty. Religious activities could benefit at times from government sponsorship, yet this support was always sufficiently unpredictable that those most interested in religion were unwilling to let their activities become entirely dependent on such funding.

A similar argument can probably be made concerning the much-noted ambivalence of religious organizations themselves toward higher education. On the one hand, most of the old-line Protestant denominations as well as the Catholic church have been responsible for the founding of numerous private colleges and universities. On the other hand, the administrators and faculties of these institutions of higher learning often found themselves in tension with their supporting ecclesiastical entities, feeling themselves pressured to take stands on issues that defied reason or that compromised their intellectual integrity. These misgivings were often justified by the presence of trustees or denominational administrators who in fact wanted to channel higher education toward their own purposes or who, in other cases, were fundamentally suspicious of the academic life in the first place. The result was a kind of uncertainty, much like that inspired by the varying interpretations of the First Amendment, and this uncertainty encouraged the various actors to seek mutually beneficial relations wherever possible and yet to maintain the relative autonomy of their respective institutions. In the larger scheme of things, religious ideas may thus have been facilitated better at many church-related colleges and universities than if denominational leaders had had complete control or no control at all.

The other resource that has perhaps had similar consequences for the role of religion in higher education is the cultural division of knowledge into disciplinary categories. This division has, on the one hand, resulted in a kind of intellectual fragmentation, and even warfare, that has often been decried by religionists who favor closer integration between, for example, theology and science or religion and the arts. The same division, on the other hand, has made it possible for ideas in these various realms to be pursued intensively in a way that would likely have been compromised had cross-disciplinary connections always been necessary. The clearest example of this positive benefit of disciplinary specialization is the fact that practitioners of the natural sciences, in which the scientific paradigm is most clearly articulated, are much more likely to retain deep personal religious convictions than are practitioners of the social sciences and the humanities, in which both the internal paradigm and external boundaries defining each discipline are less clearly articulated.

The upshot of these counterintuitive considerations is that gloomy assertions about the long-term decline of religion within higher education are probably overstated. Certainly the overall cultural climate in contemporary societies may be more heavily influenced by secular higher education than by the church, compared with the cultural climate of five hundred years ago. But the rising influence of higher education, even in its most secular forms, has also opened new opportunities for religion to influence the public sphere as part of the legitimate activities associated with colleges and universities. In addition, cultural boundaries restricting the role of religion and demarcating the sacred from the secular have not always had purely negative implications for the public expression of the sacred.

My second general question is: How does Christian higher education manifest the sacred? It is easy enough to enumerate the various programs, ministries, courses, publishing activities and the like by which religious values are made manifest through institutions of higher learning, yet to understand the nature of this process we must ask other questions. How are these values shaped by their being produced in the context of higher learning? What gives them an appearance of being sacred? How do they interact with other values that may also embody a sense of the sacred? We can seek answers to these questions by considering how the academic context constrains the public expression of the sacred and how this context also facilitates these expressions.

One of the most serious constraints on expressions of the sacred within academic contexts is the separation of reason from emotion and from action which generally characterizes institutions of higher learning. This separation reflects the lingering dualistic epistemology of the Enlightenment that presumes knowledge to be gained best by objectifying the world, viewing it as an externality, rather than attempting to appropriate it subjectively (or internally) through the counsels of feeling or through wisdom gained from direct action. While there have been significant philosophical challenges to this perspective in the 20th century, it certainly prevails in secular and church-related colleges and universities alike.

Understanding may be enriched through subjective identification with the object or by the intuitive insight gained through direct participation, but the primary goal is gaining knowledge that can be understood cognitively and communicated rationally.

Knowledge gained this way presents a special limitation for public manifestations of the sacred, for such knowledge comes across as having too little to do with the full life of the individual. Passion, trust, conviction, faith, devotion — are all subordinated to dispassionate statements about the facts or truths of a world viewed as it were from outside. It is little wonder, then, that church bureaucrats concerned with running institutions on the basis of rationally devised technical considerations have looked more to the studies and methods of academicians (especially in the social sciences) than have people in the pew who are trying to integrate faith into the full measure of their lives. For them, the words of a priest who has struggled with the same issues are likely to be meaningful in a way that an objective study of religious institutions can never be.

This observation lends some credence to the view that scholarly approaches to religion are inevitably corrosive, contributing in subtle ways to the larger processes of secularization. For the believer, depersonalized knowledge presented in scholarly texts is likely to seem alien, setting up a boundary between such knowledge (viewed as public information) and the more private insights that govern his or her spiritual life. The spiritual realm is thus increasingly segmented from public discourse, leaving it to hold mastery only over the private or subjective realm. For the nonbeliever who already approaches spirituality as a stranger looking in from the outside, depersonalized knowledge (such as a study of religious belief reported in the newspapers) can further enhance this estrangement by objectifying the religious realm and associating it with the other primarily through intellect.

A second, but related, limitation of higher education in producing the sacred derives from the tension between what might be called creation, on the one hand, and discovery, on the other hand. Creation implies invention, novelty, the development of something new that in a deep sense reflects the talents and insights of the creator. Discovery, in contrast, implies paying close attention to the external world, grasping it as a given reality, so that what is new is only a description of what has always been there. Western religion has always distinguished the two by attributing creation to a divine being who is the author or originator of all reality, whereas discovery is more likely to be described as a human activity, such as learning to understand better the nature of created reality or gaining insight into the darker recesses of one's own nature.

At the dawn of the scientific revolution, the work of scientists was well described as an act of discovery. Natural laws inscribed in the world by its creator were there for the finding, just as new continents had been there a century earlier for the explorers. Academic work was in fact likened to reading a text — in one case the text might still be the written Bible, in other cases it was the word of God written in nature. Reportage of academic discoveries was thus largely a matter of communicating knowledge of a sacred realm that was already in place. This congruity between academic work and the sacred served well to legitimate the religious sponsorship of higher learning in church-related academies and the close connections that were drawn between moral philosophy and natural philosophy in secular institutions.

The present understanding of academic work, however, has shifted decidedly away from discovery toward creation itself. Artistic expression, in which a product is created that reflects the artist's moods and interests, is perhaps the clearest model of this understanding. Increasingly, science imitates art in this respect, as measuring devices are known to alter the very realities they seek to measure and as theoretical inventions are understood to alter the very possibilities of perceiving reality. The most highly valued academic work, therefore, is the creative process by which new ideas, new theories or even new ways of expressing ideas are invented; by comparison, discovery is increasingly relegated to the realm of empiricism, fact-mongering and technical specialization.

The limitation that this conception of academic work presents for the discussion of religion is that God remains fundamentally an entity to be discovered, rather than one to be invented. Scriptural exegesis becomes a process of discovering insights within a closely circumscribed field of textual meanings and of applying these insights to changing circumstances. Going beyond discovery to create an entirely new conception of God is, however, to move beyond the place of most confessional traditions. The resultant strain between these two modes of understanding reveals itself, therefore, either as heterodoxy confronting orthodoxy or as more highly valued creative expressions confronting the less highly valued processes of textual interpretation.

The main consequence of these two limitations — depersonalized reason and the devaluation of discovery — for the public manifestation of religion through academic organizations is that academicians tend to talk about religion in ways that are seldom valued highly within their institutions themselves, while the most creative contributions to spirituality come largely from outside these institutions. What a typical lay person might read in the newspapers would thus be a report of an academic study of the religious beliefs of the American population, but this reader would not expect to learn that a fundamental new theory of God had been produced or that the authors of such a report had won a Nobel Prize for their efforts. Nor would this reader be likely to rely on such a report for guidance in his or her own attempts to seek God. Higher credence would be given to a playwright who wrote more from the deep anguish of having been imprisoned by a totalitarian government, a recovering alcoholic who had struggled with the depths of personal pain, or in the rare instance an academic marginal to any specific department or discipline who wrote more from personal reflection than from systematic empirical inquiry.

Part of the reason why discourse about the sacred would be shaped more deeply by nonacademics than by academics, if this argument is correct, is that higher learning has erected a boundary not only between reason and emotion but also between knowledge and moral discourse. The public pronouncements of academicians are more likely to take the form of descriptive statements than normative prescriptions, in part because of the way in which the role of the academy has come to be understood in modern societies. This role involves a deliberate retreat from active engagement in public life in order to protect the purity of scholarship itself. It also grants government organizations ultimate authority for the manipulation of social structures, taking only a detached advisory role in policy-making. But the fact that government in democratic societies generally refrains from intruding on the private decisions of individuals leaves a large realm untutored either by government or the academy. This realm, often described as personal morality, has always been subject to the pronouncements of religious institutions, either at the level of congregations or hierarchies.

As long as these organizations functioned with cultural authority, and when higher education consisted mainly of church-related organizations, a natural division of labor existed which allowed the academies to focus (in the best circumstances) on moral philosophy rather than on concrete moral prescriptions. With the erosion of the churches' authority over the lives of many people in modern societies, however, a gap has been created in moral discourse that seems to be filled more from common sense, ad hoc and situational reasoning, television, and other purveyors of moral fiction than by institutions of higher learning.

Rather than simply attributing this failure on the part of academicians to address moral issues to a lack of nerve or to shortsightedness of vision, we must try to understand it in terms of the kind of authority modern culture confers on academicians. Their authority as culture producers inheres mainly in the special advantages assumed to derive from specialized, critical reflection. The point of academic institutions is, after all, to provide opportunities for such reflection, and the fact that resources flow to these institutions both reinforces and attests to the legitimacy such reflection has acquired. Scholars who are interested in religious and moral questions are thus most likely to be given credence for analytic and critical studies. Taking their cue from the natural sciences, they may try to understand how the sacred functions — why it works or does not work — but in analyzing the divine in this way, they are more likely to recognize that they are examining human assumptions about God, rather than being able to observe God directly. Their authority as dispassionate scholars is likely as well to encourage critical orientations, rather than the sort of celebrations of the divine one might expect from a liturgist or a poet.

Scholars' views of nature also suggest another limitation on the kind of authoritative knowledge they may be able to produce about the sacred. These views are heavily oriented toward technical mastery and manipulation. The rationale for much of the funding that goes toward applied research, and even for basic science, is that the knowledge gained will help us better to control the physical environment. The prospect of government's being able to engage in social engineering has encouraged a similar technical orientation in the social sciences. Even in the humanities much of what passes for historical studies and literary criticism has a manipulative orientation, either in the sense of better mastering the future by knowing the past or discovering the techniques by which meaning can be created and deciphered in literature. At one time, of course, the shamans who preceded modern academicians concerned themselves largely with the technical manipulation of the gods. But in modern societies this technical orientation is largely in disrepute. Scholars may legitimately concern themselves with manipulating nature, but not God. That function has thus been given over to the various television preachers, prayer warriors, and mediums who claim specialized talents in influencing the divine. Academicians, as we have observed, are more likely to contribute to public discourse about the manipulation of religious institutions than of the sacred itself.

One other limitation of the academy deserving mention is the fact that the secular knowledge it produces is often shrouded in such sacred conceptions that this knowledge — and its pursuit — take the place of religious conviction. Anyone familiar with the capital fund-raising drives and alumni relations of colleges and universities will immediately grasp this point.

Institutions of higher learning symbolize a sacred space — the navel of the world — where truth is closer, where the mundane concerns of business and family can be bracketed from view, where athletic prowess and physical beauty are at their peak, and where the youthfulness even of aging professors and alumni can be preserved safely. If the pursuit of knowledge is in some way a sacred quest, it is all the more so because of the special places (we call them "hallowed halls") in which learning takes place. Religious congregations have an advantage over these institutions insofar as they are able to lay down the foundational values learned in early childhood.

But higher education enjoys an enormous competitive advantage over congregations in being able to capture the full-time attention of young people just at the moment when they are questioning their childhood values and adopting the ideas they will carry into adulthood. If religious ideas are fully integrated into the formal and hidden curricula of the campus, this advantage can work to the benefit of public religion. But studies documenting negative relations between the attainment of higher education and the retention of religious convictions suggest a different pattern. Campuses may delegitimate religion both by subjecting it to critical reason and by sanctifying alternative values, such as relativism, the pursuit of secular knowledge for its own sake, or even raw careerism, narrow professionalism, and crass materialism.

These limitations notwithstanding, the campus environment also enjoys certain features that contribute positively to the public manifestation of the sacred. One of the most important of these is the atmosphere of open, unrestrained intellectual inquiry that is often associated with higher education. Just how open this atmosphere actually is has been questioned repeatedly in recent years, especially by critics who argue that higher education is dominated by a subtle but powerful liberal ideology that prevents genuine consideration of politically or religiously conservative perspectives. Compared to many other institutional settings there is, nevertheless, a relatively strong norm in the academic environment against imposing explicit ideological tests on the activities of those who are engaged in serious intellectual pursuits.

The upshot is that students and faculty often find the academy a more conducive setting in which to engage in frank explorations of religious values than virtually anywhere else. In contrast, the same person may feel uncomfortable in a congregational setting, for example, because certain answers are assumed to be precluded from the outset or because clergy function not only as spiritual guides, but as commandeers of volunteer labor and charitable donation. Secular campuses probably convey the image of being most open to exploring issues, including religious ones, from all angles with nothing other than genuine intellectual integrity at stake. However, this image often does fall short of reality because of ingrained prejudices against the value of faith or the wisdom of religious traditions themselves. Church-related campuses may preclude some of the freedom to explore from all possible angles because of their loyalty to particular traditions, yet this limitation may be more than compensated for by the seriousness with which the religious life itself is taken.

In attempting to communicate the results of these explorations to the wider public, scholars in these various settings are likely to experience similar advantages and disadvantages. The main advantage accruing to the scholar in a secular academic setting is that whatever conclusions the scholar chooses to publicize may be accorded the respect that comes with a presumably objective approach. The disadvantage is that a deeply impassioned plea, framed in a confessional language by such a scholar, is likely to earn trouble for that person within the academy itself. For scholars at church-related colleges, the obverse is likely to pertain: Trust may be granted only by an audience sharing the same confessional tradition, but speaking passionately from this tradition is less likely to be regarded as a breach of academic norms.

The technical or applied knowledge mentioned earlier also gives institutions of higher learning some clear advantages in influencing the shape of religious institutions. Scholars may find it beyond their legitimate roles to invent new gods or to manipulate existing gods, but they can produce knowledge which the leaders of religious hierarchies take seriously enough to influence the direction of these hierarchies. Studies of how the churches promoted anti-Semitism were at one point influential, for example, in encouraging church leaders to adopt different official policies toward Jews. Studies in more recent years documenting that congregations were able fairly readily to accept women in clergy roles have been instrumental in encouraging denominational leaders to champion gender equality in the churches.

Finally, let us look for a moment at the question: What are the prospects for church-related institutions of higher learning to manifest the sacred in the future? Much of what I have already discussed will continue to apply in the decades to come. But there is another opportunity to be considered as well. Probably the greatest challenge in American religion to which academic knowledge can respond positively in the years ahead is the growing level of religious and cultural pluralism that characterizes our society. Although pluralism has sometimes been thought to lead inevitably toward greater secularity, the future of religion in pluralistic societies is probably more indeterminate than that view would suggest. Pluralism can stimulate competition among religious traditions, and it can be layered into deeper personal religious convictions as well.

Academic knowledge has for several centuries advanced the cause of cultural pluralism, claiming to present a more enlightened vantage point than that available within any particular tradition, and championing egalitarianism, mutual respect, and the search for shared values among pluralistic subcultures. Academic knowledge has continuously been put forth in universalistic terms said to be relevant and applicable in a wide variety of settings.

Arguments couched in universalistic language serve a vital function in public discourse about collective values. Indeed, it might be argued that the chief role to be played by higher education in manifesting the sacred is that of arbiter or translator, framing arguments in detached, externalist terms so that they can be understood and debated across a wide spectrum of confessional traditions. Congregations, denominational hierarchies and religious special interest groups may also do this in their efforts to reach pluralistic audiences, but colleges and universities are in a better position to do so because they do not speak from the perspective of any particular religious tradition.

Church-related colleges are of course somewhat more constrained in this than are secular institutions of higher learning, but many church-related colleges have been able to devise charters giving themselves sufficient autonomy from host denominations so that faculty and students still have relatively wide latitude in exploring intellectual questions. Academicians in both types of settings have the cultural authority to raise critical questions and to pose religious issues in broader — historical, cross-cultural and cross-confessional — terms so that these issues can genuinely become part of the wider public culture. Being able to speak *about* religious language, rather than having to speak *in* religious language itself, is of special value when competing religious arguments are at issue.

On balance, then, the view that colleges and universities necessarily are subject to, and contributors to, a secularized public culture seems mistaken, just as does the view that colleges and universities must tighten their ties to sponsoring religious bodies if they are going to resist these secularizing pressures. Secularization misconstrues the question, because it suggests a linear trend away from something definably religious toward something patently nonreligious. A more compelling view of the changes taking place in modern societies is one that recognizes the simultaneous interplay of the sacred and the secular. Colleges and universities have contributed significantly — and will continue to contribute — to this interplay. They are among the chief producers of secular knowledge. But they also provide valuable enclaves in which special types of religious knowledge can be produced and preserved.

ENDNOTES

1. Portions of this chapter are contained in the work *Producing the Sacred: An Essay on Public Religion* by Robert Wuthnow (Urbana: University of Illinois Press, 1994). Used by permission of the University of Illinois Press.
2. Robert Wuthnow, *The Restructuring of American Religion: Society & Faith Since World War II* (Princeton, NJ: Princeton University Press, 1990).

CHAPTER 9
Christian Higher Education: The Church at the Frontlines of the Culture

Steve Moore

It was Thomas Kuhn who aptly reminded us that paradigm shifts are usually acknowledged and accepted only after many years of anxiety, ambiguity and even antagonism.[1] That change is a part of the human experience, and that we are slow to recognize, admit or assimilate the realities of paradigmatic change in our lives, our culture and our world comes as no surprise. As Woody Allen has quipped, "History repeats itself. It has to. Nobody listens the first time around."

Our institutions, the church, the family, the government, etc., provide key roles in our lives as we seek to negotiate, understand and incorporate change. But our institutions are also subject to change. They too must grow and adapt or they will die or become irrelevant. The challenge for the Christian and for Christian institutions is how to change and grow without accommodating and assimilating the values of the culture around us. What many leaders from within and outside of the church have observed is that for more than a generation there has been a general tendency within the church and her institutions to withdraw from genuine engagement with the culture and the ideas shaping the culture. The reasons for this withdrawal are many and complex and are as much a result of being pushed out of "the public square" as intentional departure.

Having lost the battle to be a major influence in the culture, most in the church have accepted the relegation of Christian faith to the private sector, where it can influence the choices of those who participate. The tragedy of such a decision, Lesslie Newbigin concludes, is that:

> ... the awesome and winsome claim of Jesus Christ to be alone the Lord of all the world, the light that alone shows the whole of reality as it really is, the life that alone endures forever — this claim is effectively silenced. It [Christianity] remains, for our culture, just one of the varieties of religious experience.[2]

However, it will be as we seek to re-emerge from privatized faith that we gain the ability to fulfill our calling as "salt" and "light" in a world desperately in need of both. As well, it is the university, which stands at the frontlines of the culture, that is in a great position to serve the church in the critique of the culture and to contribute to the equipping of Christians for lives of engagement as transformation agents. Let me suggest six facets of the current cultural milieu that provide a challenge to which Christian higher education must respond in an increasingly effective manner if we are to fulfill our mission and advance the work of the kingdom.

The first challenge facing Christian higher education is the dominant influence of a technological, mechanistic view of the world which permeates our work and life. Frederick Winslow Taylor is hardly a household name. Yet his influence has shaped all of our lives from the schoolhouse to the workplace. Taylor, who lived from 1856-1915, is better known in business circles as the father of scientific management, perhaps one of the first of this century's "efficiency experts." Taylor believed that every task could be broken into component parts and reassembled into a tightly controlled and regimented form. He believed that human work was simply the sum of a series of well-ordered parts. "In the past man has been first, in the future systems will be first," Taylor proclaimed.[3]

Taylor's analysis of how work is done became the foundation for assembly lines, the 40-hour work week, the 50-minute class period, etc. Peter Drucker calls his work "the most powerful and most lasting contribution an

American has made to Western thought since the Federalist papers."[4]

Despite such unrestrained praise, Taylor has also been criticized because his work tends to devalue the common workers and relegate them to "institutional parts" controlled by a managerial elite. His desire to make efficiency a central driving value of the 21st century has impacted us in many ways, not the least of which is a view of education as merely the accumulation of knowledge. While Taylor was not alone in promoting such views, his work helped promote a reductionist view of humankind where people were thought of as machines. His views also undermined the Christian notion of "vocation" or "calling" as a central part of our understanding of what it means to be human. Once severed, the connection between work and values — such as dignity, purpose, service, creativity and artistry — was lost.

Some have also suggested that as we have increasingly seen the world as mechanistic, technology has emerged as a major influence upon our understanding of communication and culture. There is little doubt that humankind has benefited in significant ways from the remarkable advances technology achieved. Yet the rapid developments in technology also seem to have mesmerized and hypnotized the culture with loads of information and information access. The danger is that as we adapt ourselves to the vast lateral connectedness made possible through technology, we are tempted to give up on our search for depth and wisdom. We must remember it is wisdom that has been one of the central forces motivating humankind's advances. It is wisdom that answers the "so what" of a zillion gigabytes of information. We must celebrate and encourage technology's advances and contributions and recognize its inadequacies to answer life's most important questions.

The second challenge presented by our culture is the superficiality and futility created by media-dominated public discourse.

We sometimes fail to grasp the incongruity created when a new celebrity anchorperson reports in one breath that "10,000 people died of hunger in some African country today" and in the next breath encourages us to brush our teeth or choose our deodorant carefully. Such a disjointed view of the world, coupled with direct mail, talk radio and instant worldwide news results in a media barrage that produces "information overload" and "compassion fatigue."

In his work *Before the Shooting Begins*, James Davidson Hunter suggests the main problem of the press is not bias (though inevitably there is bias — most in the press are unaware of their biases) but superficiality.[5] Most in the media are unable or unwilling to move beyond framing all issues in a polarized, protagonist/antagonist manner. As this carries over to the church, it undermines our ability to deal with the complexities and realities of everyday life. Critical issues are presented in simplistic forms: One is either pro-abortion or against it; you are either pro-homosexual or homophobic. There is no room for the nuances and difficulties of real human situations.

In his commencement address at Catholic University, media "insider" Ted Koppell addressed this by saying:

> We have actually convinced ourselves that slogans will save us. Shoot up, if you must, but use a clean needle. Enjoy sex whenever and with whomever you wish, but wear a condom. "No." The answer is "No." Not because it isn't cool or smart or because you might end up in jail or dying in an AIDS ward, but "No" because it's wrong, because we have spent 5,000 years as a race of rational human beings trying to drag ourselves out of the primeval slime by searching for truth and moral absolutes. In the place of truth, we have discovered facts. For moral absolutes, we have substituted moral ambiguity. We now communicate with everyone and say absolutely nothing. We have reconstructed the Tower of Babel, and it is a television antenna: *a thousand voices producing a daily parody of democracy, in which everyone's opinion is afforded equal weight regardless of substance or merit.* Indeed, it can even be argued that opinions of real weight tend to sink with barely a trace in television's ocean of banalities. Our society finds truth too strong a medicine to digest undiluted. *In its purest form, truth is not a polite tap on the shoulder. It*

is a howling reproach.[6] [Emphasis mine]

In the face of futility and superficiality, Christian higher education must inspire and encourage hope. It is perhaps a modern tendency to think of hope as passive, "pie in the sky," or wishful thinking. Instead we need to reclaim an understanding of hope as described by one early church father who proclaimed, "Hope has two daughters: Anger and Courage. Anger with the way things are, courage to change them." Or as Croatian theologian Peter Kuzmic has beautifully explained, "Hope is the ability to listen to the music of the future. Faith is the courage to dance to it in the present."[7]

The third challenge facing Christian higher education is the "psychological-therapeutic" mindset held almost as an unofficial religion of the culture. In his work *The Triumph of the Therapeutic: Uses of Faith After Freud*, Phillip Reiff points out how psychotherapy is not simply a tool for helping individuals, but rather the engine of a cultural revolution that has implications far wider than individual clients.[8] While I want to affirm the contributions and benefits gained from psychology, counseling and therapy, as Christians we need to reclaim the healing power of "Koinonia" and "metanoia" in the ongoing work of the Holy Spirit.

Said another way, psychology is a good servant to our understanding of being human but a bad master. In developing our understanding of what it means to be human, we need to let the norm of the person of Jesus Christ become our model for wholeness instead of letting our pathologies become the defining criteria of personhood. I understand that one could easily misconstrue what is being said as "anti-therapeutic" or resistant to the insights of psychology (or even that my inner child is rebelling ...). Nothing could be further from the truth. What I am suggesting, rather, is that we strengthen and expand our understanding of ecclesiology (the mission of the church) and Christology (the person of Christ). As research has frequently shown, for most people the most significant healing and support come from being part of a vital, healthy fellowship which focuses upon worship, service, outreach and celebration rather than becoming individually focused on dysfunction.

Eugene Peterson reminds us that:

> We human beings learn early and quickly to acquire expertise in using our plight, whatever it is, ... in getting our own way. This impulse to make oneself the center, to shrewdly or bullyingly manipulate things and people to the service of self is what we call sin ... a great deal of caring is simply collaboration in selfishness, in self-pity, in self-destruction, in self-indulgence — all the seemingly endless hyphenations that the self is able to engineer.[9]

Christian higher education would serve the church and our students well by helping them understand that the sense of alienation and malaise many people experience may not be the effect of individual experiences, but the result of living in a culture that fosters alienation in multiple ways. This would include but not be limited to the impact of modern scientism, rationalism, technology and the multimedia frenzy.[10]

As Christian higher education seeks to educate and equip students for engagement with the world, we would make a significant contribution by encouraging a sense of the holy, the sacred. We serve students well by inviting them into and having them fully participate in learning communities where the wonder and beauty of creation and the healing power of love and truth are celebrated and experienced.

The fourth challenge for Christian higher education as it prepares to enter the 21st century is the need to develop an apologetic for a postmodern way of thinking. This would include both an ability to understand the presuppositions of the competing worldviews and the ability to present a sound and thoughtful reason for our faith. We live in a world increasingly lacking in an ability to discern true from false, legitimate from counterfeit. Though sometimes a myth circulates that our culture is totally secular, nothing could be further from the truth. While "institutional religion" often experiences opposition, spiritualities of every sort flourish. We live in a religiously pluralistic, pagan society. I have often observed that there are two central and sacred commitments in contemporary culture:

1. It doesn't matter what you believe as long as you are sincere.

2. One can believe anything one wants as long as it does not place any demands on the way I live or make any judgments on how I live, and as long as one keeps what one believes to oneself.

Both of these cultural commitments are false. Sincerity has never been and never will be a test of truth. Faith, while certainly personal, is not a private matter.

Perhaps there is no greater example of the fallacy and consequence of this thinking than the life and death of Kurt Cobain of the grunge rock group Nirvana. While he was admired for his vulnerability and raw honesty, his life was anchored to a lie that eventually took him under. In writings found after his suicide he said, "I haven't felt excitement in listening to as well as creating music ... for too many years now. The fact is I can't fool you, any of you. It simply isn't fair to you or to me. The worst crime I can think of would be to put people off by faking it and pretending as if I was having 100 percent fun."[11] In spite of some popular opinion, the goal of life is not having 100 percent fun or even pretending you are. The goal is to give our heart, soul, mind and strength to God and to give ourselves to the purposes of His kingdom!

In 1939, T.S. Eliot gave a series of lectures on "Christianity and Culture." In them he describes what he believes to be the epochs of modern Western history and the ways in which Christianity has been presented in them. Regardless of what the next epoch holds, Eliot warns, "... it is important and essential that we not revert to a very dangerous inversion where we advocate Christianity not because it is true but because it might be beneficial."[12] He continues by stating:

It is not enthusiasm but dogma that differentiates a Christian from a Pagan society. We must first know and proclaim the truth of Christianity before we commend the necessity of morality (Christian life) ... Only God can give ultimate purpose to our lives and direction to our society. The Ten Commandments are not just a text to be memorized by a literate class, they are the basis for a just and humane society.[13]

While our students must learn discernment and understand the nature and importance of what is true, they must be able to understand and navigate in a world increasingly pluralistic in its religious orientation. Different religions cannot be dismissed as "pagan" or accepted as merely another of the many paths to God.

In a conversation with Tenzin Gyatso, the 14th Dalai Lama, I once asked, "There are those in Christianity and Buddhism who would say that our faiths are simply different ways of saying the same thing — How would you respond?" He got very animated and replied:

> We must not fool ourselves — the teachings of Buddhism and Christianity are fundamentally different and in some cases at odds. We must not mask our differences or play as if they are not there. However, there are many ways we can work together to feed the sick, house the homeless, shelter the orphans, and clothe the naked. Where we can, we must work together. Where we differ we must honestly say so.[14]

In our eagerness to be open we sometimes have given the impression it doesn't matter what one believes. We must recover a Christian apologetic that is winsome, engaging and nondefensive.

The fifth challenge in the "spirit of the age" that must be addressed is the cultural obsession with sexuality as the defining characteristic of our humanness. From gay-rights activists who raise and spend millions to convince us their lifestyle is acceptable, to the constant bombardment of the media which portrays sex as the essence of relationships, to the radical fundamentalist who condemns people and actions alike without understanding either, we live in a world inundated with half-truths and self-justifying excuses.

I discovered a great insight on this from G.K. Chesterton who said, "The man who knocks at the door of the brothel is looking for God."[15]

At first I thought, *How could he say that a person about to patronize a house of prostitution is looking for God?* Then I realized Chesterton was making an observation of great insight. Underlying the man's quest for "purchased sex" was really a quest for intimacy. Chesterton's challenge to us is to probe beneath the surface motivations of our culture, and we will find in all cases — as Augustine has said, "Our hearts are restless until they find their rest in thee."

Our hunger to know and to be known has led us into a cultural preoccupation with defining humanity by sexuality. This can be seen in "new Puritanism" on campuses across the country. A reductionistic and legalistic understanding of human relationships and sexuality is being promoted where students are given little guidance in the mystery and dynamic of human relationships. The relational contract codes and "training" and "education" which characterize this "new Puritanism" take a mechanistic view of sex. Condoms are distributed, and students are encouraged to practice "safe sex" with little if any discussion of the consequences of serial sexual intimacy.

When the runaway best seller *Bridges of Madison County* came out as a movie, a controversy ensued when viewers discovered it was a fictional story — not based on a true story as many had hoped and supposed. People were devastated and angry. They wanted the romance, the love, the intimacy, the caring to be true. It struck a chord within the culture. It resonated with the hunger present in all of us for authenticity in love and life, and for the desire to be completely open and giving to another. It is the desire to know and be known, to be fully human and fully alive.

Paul Brand, now in his 80s, made some very interesting comments in this regard at the dedication of a new retirement facility. Brand is a famous hand surgeon who also developed innovative techniques for the treatment of leprosy. He, with Philip Yancey, wrote *Fearfully and Wonderfully Made*, a beautiful work on the mystery of the human body. At the dedication Brand reflected:

> I remember well when I was at my physical peak. I was 27. I felt completely at comfort with my body. I was in excellent physical condition and my body felt finely tuned. I realize now that for

many, after reaching that peak, the rest of their life is downhill. I also remember well, like yesterday, my intellectual peak. I was 58 years of age. I was perhaps at my peak professionally as a surgeon. All of my training came together and felt as if my skills were finely tuned. I realize now that for many, after reaching that peak, the rest of their life is downhill. I am now in my 80s. I realize that I am fast approaching my spiritual peak. It can be the place where everything comes together around compassion, kindness, wisdom and love. I realize that I will not cross that peak nor am I soon to head downhill, for I am entering into the fullness of what it means to be human and that is part of the reality that we as Christians enjoy in God's gift of eternity.[16]

Now that is a view of what it means to be human! It reflects a wisdom about "personhood" that dwarfs our culture's shallow views of humanity defined primarily by sexuality and offers an enduring and inviting perspective on life. It is an understanding of our humanity rooted in Genesis. It should also be a principle component of higher learning that calls itself Christian.

Finally, I would suggest that Christian higher education should challenge the culture and offer its students a sense of connection with the past. At times one gets a sense of "cultural chauvinism" in the attitudes of the late 20th century. Individuals in the "current age" look down on previous generations and other cultures as "unenlightened" and "boorish" because they fail to exhibit the cultural mores of today.

Noah Ben Shea, a poet and storyteller, has a way of illustrating important themes in helpful ways. He tells a parable of children, circuses and giants that brings this issue into focus.

A Giant or a Burden?

After dinner, the children turned to Jacob and asked if he would tell them a story. "A story about what?" asked Jacob.

"About a giant," squealed the children.

Jacob smiled, leaned against the warm stones at the side of the fireplace, and began, his voice turning softly inward.

"Once there was a boy who asked his father to take him to see the great parade that passed through the village where they lived. The father, remembering the parade from when he was a boy, quickly agreed, and the next morning the boy and his father set out together.

"As they approached the route the parade would take, people started to push in from all sides, and the crowd grew thick. When the people along the way became almost a wall, the father lifted his son and placed him on his shoulders.

"Soon the parade began, and as it passed, the boy kept telling his father how wonderful it was, how spectacular were the colors and images. The boy, in fact, grew so prideful of what he saw that he mocked those who saw less, saying even to his father, 'If only you could see what I see.'"

"But," said Jacob, staring straight into the faces of the children, "what the boy did not look at was *why* he could see. What the boy forgot was that once his father, too, could see."

Then, as if he had finished the story, Jacob stopped speaking and simply looked at the fire. The children turned to Jacob, showing disappointment at how the story had ended.

"Is that it?" said the girl. "We thought you were going to tell us a story about a giant."

"But I did," said Jacob, smiling, watching how silence invited expectation. "I told you a story about a boy who *could* have been a giant."

"How?" squealed the children.

"A giant," said Jacob, "is anyone who remembers we are all sitting on someone else's shoulders."

"And what does it make us if we don't remember?" asked the boy.

"A burden," answered Jacob.[17]

The time has come to begin a new chapter in telling the story of Christian higher education. The opportunity is at hand to join the purpose and passion of the past to the progress of the present and create an exciting future. Will our colleges and universities make a significant, eternal impact on the lives of students in the world of higher education, in the life of our communities, our country, our world? Or will our institutions take the bland predictable road of American private higher education and merely attempt to mimic the latest trends, whatever they may be?

To paraphrase some thoughts once expressed by Father Henri Nouwen, the church and the world are in need of Christians educated and prepared to reflect on the painful and joyful realities of every day with the "mind of Jesus." By so doing, they can in turn elevate our human experience to the reality and knowledge of God's gentle guidance and transforming presence. That is good news to a broken, fragmented and wounded world. A college or university with that kind of mission is truly about the business of educating for the kingdom.

ENDNOTES

1. Thomas Kuhn, *The Structure of Scientific Revolution*, 2nd Edition (Chicago: University of Chicago Press, 1970).

2. Lesslie Newbigin, *Foolishness to the Greeks* (Grand Rapids: Eerdmans, 1986).

3. Robert Kanigel, *The One Best Way: Frederick Winslow Taylor and the Enigma of Efficiency* (New York: Viking Press, 1997).

4. The Mars Hill Tapes, Volume 27 (Summer 1997). Charlottesville, VA.

5. James Davidson Hunter, *Before the Shooting Begins: Searching for Democracy in America's Culture War* (New York: Free Press, 1994).

6. Ted Koppell, Commencement Address, Catholic University, Washington, D.C. (May 1994).

7. Peter Kuzmic, Commencement Address, Seattle Pacific University, Seattle, WA (June 1993).

8. Philip Reiff, *The Triumph of the Therapeutic: Uses of Faith After Freud* (Chicago: University of Chicago Publishers, 1987).

9. Eugene Peterson, *Subversive Spirituality* (Grand Rapids: Eerdmans, 1995).

10. An excellent resource examining this issue is an interview with Dr. Paul McCugh, "Psychiatry and the Spirit of the Age" Mars Hill Conversations, 1996. Charlottesville, VA.

11. *Seattle Times*. April 11, 1994, Section B, p. 1.

12. T.S. Eliot, *The Idea of a Christian Society* (New York: Harcourt Brace, 1960, c 1949).

13. Ibid.

14. Steve Moore, Unpublished remarks of the Dalai Lama, Dharmsala India, 1985.

15. G.K. Chesterton, *Collected Works IV* (San Francisco: Ignatius Press, 1987).

16. Steve Moore, Unpublished remarks of Paul Brand, Seattle, WA: 1995.

17. Noah Ben Shea, *Jacob's Journey* (New York: Ballantine Books, 1984).